Cambridge Primary

C000261084

Hodder Cambridge Primary

Maths

Learner's Book

Stage 6

Chris Baker

with Steph King and Josh Lury

Series editors: Mike Askew and Paul Broadbent

HODDER
EDUCATION
AN HACHETTE UK COMPANY

Author acknowledgements

With warm thanks to Jennifer Peek for her help in shaping and developing this title.

The Publisher is extremely grateful to the following schools for their comments and feedback during the development of this series:

Avalon Heights World Private School, Ajman

The Oxford School, Dubai

Al Amana Private School, Sharjah

British International School, Ajman

Wesgreen International School, Sharjah

As Seeb International School, Al Khoud.

Photograph acknowledgements

We would like to thank the following for their permission to reproduce photographs:

p.12 © Lisa Werner/Alamy Stock Photo; **p.54** (all) © Hachette UK; **p.68** © Graeme Dawes/Shutterstock; **p.70** *l* © Aaron Amat/Shutterstock; **p.70** *r* © Talvi/Shutterstock; **p.85** © Tim Hester/123rf; **p.102** *t* © Newmaster/Shutterstock; **p.102** *c* © Transia Design/Shutterstock; **p.102** *r* © Mixfree/Shutterstock; **p.116** © Konstantin Chagin/123rf; **p.117** tl © Chaoss/Shutterstock; **p.117** tr © Simone Caltabiano/Shutterstock; **p.117** *bl* © Stillfx/Shutterstock; **p.117** *br* © Helen Field/Shutterstock; **p.120** © Mark Doherty/Shutterstock; **p.136** © Bowie15/123rf; **p.150** *tl* © ESB Professional/Shutterstock; **p.150** tr © Kuznetsov Alexey/Shutterstock; **p.150** *bl* © Domhnall dods/Shutterstock; **p.150** *cr* © Babaroga/Shutterstock; **p.150** *br* © Rob Bouwman/Shutterstock; **p.167** *l* © Bigjom-jom/Shutterstock; **p.167** *r* © Nechaevkon/Shutterstock; **p.169** *l* © Danita Delimont/Getty Images; **p.169** *r* © Inu/Shutterstock; **p.171** *tl* © Phil Degginger/Alamy Stock Photo; **p.171** *tr* © Wildlife Gmbh/Alamy Stock Photo; **p.171** *bl* © Stellar Gems/Shutterstock; **p.171** *br* © PNSJ88/Shutterstock.

t = top, *b* = bottom, *l* = left, *r* = right, *c* = centre

Practice test exam-style questions and sample answers are written by the author.

Every effort has been made to trace all copyright holders, but if any have been inadvertently overlooked the Publishers will be pleased to make the necessary arrangements at the first opportunity.

Although every effort has been made to ensure that website addresses are correct at time of going to press, Hodder Education cannot be held responsible for the content of any website mentioned in this book. It is sometimes possible to find a relocated web page by typing in the address of the home page for a website in the URL window of your browser.

Hachette UK's policy is to use papers that are natural, renewable and recyclable products and made from wood grown in well-managed forests and other controlled sources. The logging and manufacturing processes are expected to conform to the environmental regulations of the country of origin.

Orders: please contact Hachette UK Distribution,
Hely Hutchinson Centre, Milton Road,
Didcot, Oxfordshire, OX11 7HH. Telephone: +44 (0)1235 827827.
Email education@hachette.co.uk
Lines are open from 9 a.m. to 5 p.m., Monday to Friday.
You can also order through our website:
www.hoddereducation.com

© Chris Baker, Steph King and Josh Lury 2017

Published by Hodder Education

An Hachette UK Company

Carmelite House, 50 Victoria Embankment, London EC4Y 0DZ

Impression number   9

Year   2021

Cover illustration by Steve Evans

Illustrations by Jeanne du Plessis, Vian Oelofsen and Stephan Theron

Typeset in FS Albert 12/14 by DTP Impressions

Printed and bound by CPI Group (UK) Ltd, Croydon, CR0 4YY

A catalogue record for this title is available from the British Library

9781471884429

Contents

I am Nita.

I am Mateo.

Introduction

Explore the picture or problem.

What do you see? What can you find?

New words are in a list for you to learn.

Learn new maths skills with your teacher. Look at the diagrams to help you.

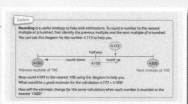

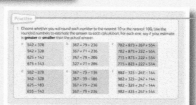

Practise the maths you have learnt. Write any answers in your exercise book.

Try this challenge activity to make you think carefully about the maths.

Read these hints and tips to help you **think like a mathematician**.

At the end of each unit try the **self-check** activities. What have you learnt?

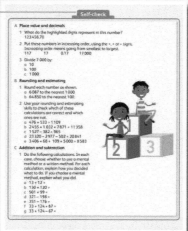

Unit 1 Number and problem solving

1a Place value and decimals

Explore

Caleb, Kim and Thandi are in the Stage 6 class with Nita and Mateo.

Caleb is trying to make the number larger each time, but Kim is trying to make it smaller. The children can swap two digits around on their turn or make a digit one larger or one smaller.

What could Caleb do next to make the number larger?

Key words

digit
greater than
hundredth
less than
million
place value
tenth

Place value in whole numbers to 1 million

Learn

1 000 000 is ten times larger than 100 000.
1 000 000 is one more than 999 999.
How many more than 999 000 is it?
How many more than 100 000 is it?

Millions	Hundred thousands	Ten thousands	Thousands	Hundreds	Tens	Units
	1	0	0	0	0	0
1	0	0	0	0	0	0
	9	9	9	9	9	9

Practise

1 Write down these numbers in words. The first one has been done for you.

  a 123 one hundred and twenty-three

  b 2 001   c 20 202   d 2 020 202

2 Write down the answers in digits.
  The first one has been done for you.

  a 10 less than three hundred and sixty-six   356

  b 10 more than one thousand

  c 99 less than one hundred thousand, two hundred

  d 500 more than nine hundred and ninety-nine thousand, five hundred

  e 500 less than one million

3 What is the value of the underlined digit each time?
  The first one has been done for you.

  a 5<u>4</u>5   40   b 5 450

  c 54 508   d 545 089

  e 455 890   f 455 890

Try this

I am thinking of a whole number. It has seven digits, and no two digits are the same.

What are the largest and smallest numbers Nita could be thinking of? What do you notice about these numbers?

Decimal places

Learn

One tenth is ten times smaller than one unit.

One hundredth is ten times smaller than one tenth, and a hundred times smaller than one unit.

Units	Tenths	Hundredths
2	4	3

This number is 2.43 and you would say 'two point four three'. It has 4 tenths and 3 hundredths.

What number is two tenths more than 2.43?

What number is three hundredths less than 2.43?

What number is five tenths and seven hundredths more than 2.43?

Practise

1   Partition these numbers to show the value of each digit.
    The first one has been done for you.

    a   6.42 = 6 + 0.4 + 0.02   b   64.25   c   64.05

    d   64.52   e   3.01   f   30.15

2   a   What number is five tenths less than 6.42?

    b   What number is nine tenths and five hundredths more than 64.05?

3   How many times larger is the digit 7 in 17.25 than the digit 7 in 15.07?

Try this

What do you think the third digit after the decimal point is called? Can you keep adding more places after that? What do you think those places are called? How can you find out?

Using symbols for greater than, less than and equal to

Learn

The equals (=), less than (<) and greater than (>) signs can be used to compare numbers or amounts.

4 tenths = 40 hundredths

This tells you that 4 tenths has the same value as 40 hundredths, so they are equal.
What can you say about each of these comparisons?

0.1 < 3   3 000 = 2 500 + 500

0.3 > 0.03   999 998 < 999 9989 < 1 000 000

Practise

1 Are these statements true or false? Correct any statements that are false.

a 10 201 = 10 210
   102.01 < 102.1
   1 020.1 > 1 020
   1 000 = 10 × 10 × 10

b 36.4 = 36.40
   3.64 < 3.46
   36 440 > 36 430.9
   36.4 = 364 ÷ 100

c 5.65 > 5.45 > 5.05
   56.5 < 55.6 < 55.5
   5 650 = 56.5 × 100
   $5^2 < 30 < 6^2$

2 Write each set of values from smallest to largest. Use the < or > symbol correctly between each pair of numbers.

a 2 354   3 245   2 345

b 243.5 km   32.45 km   234.5 km

c 758 455   785 545   78 558.5

d nine hundred thousand   1 000 000   90 001   190 100

3 Write each set of values from largest to smallest. Use the < or > symbol correctly between each pair of numbers.

a 235.4   324.5   23.45

b $2\frac{1}{2}$ kg   2.25 kg   2.1 kg

c 7 584.55   78 554.5   78 558

d $11\frac{1}{4}$ 11.01   11.75   11.2

Think like a mathematician

Remember that all fractions can be written as decimals.
What is the decimal equivalence of $\frac{1}{2}$ and $\frac{1}{4}$?

Multiplying and dividing by 10, 100 or 1000

Learn

Millions	Hundred thousands	Ten thousands	Thousands	Hundreds	Tens	Units	Tenths	Hundredths	
			3	7	5	2			
		3	7	5	2	0			3752 × 10
	3	7	5	2	0	0			3752 × 100
3	7	5	2	0	0	0			3752 × 1000

Multiplying by 10 makes a quantity ten times larger.

Multiplying by 100 makes a quantity one hundred times larger.

Multiplying by 1 000 makes a quantity one thousand times larger.

Remember that zero plays an important role because it keeps the other digits in the number in the correct place.

What do you notice about the way the digits move each time to show how the number 3 752 has been scaled?

Millions	Hundred thousands	Ten thousands	Thousands	Hundreds	Tens	Units	Tenths	Hundredths	
			3	7	5	2			
				3	7	5	2		3752 ÷ 10
					3	7	5	2	3752 ÷ 100

Dividing by 10 makes a quantity ten times smaller.

What happens to a quantity when it is divided by 100?

Can you explain what will happen to the number 10 000 when it is divided by 1 000?

Practise

1 Solve the calculations. Work down the columns.

The first one has been done for you.

a 125 × 1000   125 000

125 × 10 × 100

100 × 125

125 × 1000 ÷ 10

b 965 × 1000

9 650 × 10 × 10

9 650 ÷ 100

9 650 ÷ 1000

c 915 × 100

9 150 ÷ 10

9 151 ÷ 10

9 151 ÷ 100 × 100

2 | 325 cm | 1000 m | 55 mm | 2 km |

a Make each length 10 times longer.

b Now make each new length 100 times shorter.

c How many times shorter are the lengths now than those you started with at the beginning of question 2?

Try this

Matio weighs his pet hamster.
Its mass is 39 grams.

Nita weighs her pet cat. Its mass is 3.9 kilograms.

How many times heavier is the cat than the hamster?

1b **Rounding and estimating**

Can you **estimate** how many people are in the stadium? How can you get an **approximate** answer without having to count everybody?

Rounding and estimating

Learn

Rounding is a useful strategy to help with estimations. To round a number to the nearest multiple of a hundred, first identify the previous multiple and the next multiple of a hundred.

You can use this diagram for the number 4 172 to help you.

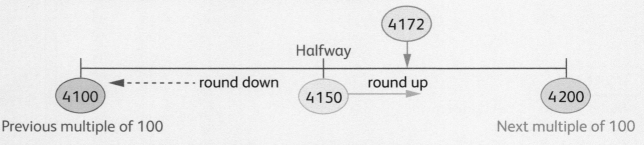

Previous multiple of 100   Next multiple of 100

Now round 4 109 to the nearest 100 using the diagram to help you.

What would be a good estimate for the calculation 4 172 + 4 109?

How will the estimate change for the same calculation when each number is rounded to the nearest 1 000?

Practise

1   Round each of these numbers.

Round to the nearest 10	Round to the nearest 100	Round to the nearest 1 000
183	649	855
1 183	6 449	8 505
10 138	64 494	18 055
13 108	64 404	18 505

2   Are these statements true or false? Correct any statements that are false.

a   264 rounds down to 270.
b   2 640 rounds down to 2 600.
c   2 640 rounds up to 3 000.
d   2 649 and 2 551 round to 2 600.
e $12 649 and $11 551 round to $12 000.
f $19 500 and $20 499 round to $20 000.

3   There are letters, A, B, C… on the number line. Each of the letters is the answer to one of the questions below. Write down the correct letter next to the question number. The first one has been done for you.

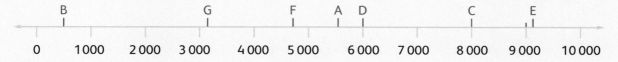

a   6 120 rounded to the nearest 1 000   6 120 rounds down to 6 000. So, the answer is D.

b   7 855 rounded to the nearest 1 000

c   The approximate position of 5 555

d   The approximate position of 500

e   Now estimate the position of the remaining letters.

1c **Addition and subtraction**

Explore

What do we get if we add up all the numbers from 1 to 100?

Is there a quick way to do this calculation?

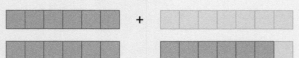

Learn

You can use number facts to help work out calculations.

For example: 6 + 6 = 12. This is a double, which you have already learnt.

So: 6 + 7 = 12 + 1 = 13
This is one more than 12.

6 + 7 is a near double.

Or, if you remember, for example:

18 + 2 = 20. This is a number bond, which you have already learnt.

20	
18	2

You can quickly work out that
18 + 3 = 18 + 2 + 1 = 20 + 1 = 21.
This is one more than 20.

Practise

1 Answer these questions using the strategies you have just learnt.

a
10 + 10
10 + 11
10 + 9

b
5 + 5
5 + 6
5 + 4

c
7 + 7
7 + 8
7 + 6

d
9 + 9
9 + 10
9 + 11

2 What are the missing numbers? The first one has been done for you.

a
13 + $\boxed{7}$ = 20
14 + ☐ = 20
☐ + 5 = 20

b
12 + 6 = ☐
13 + ☐ = 19
☐ + 6 = 20

c
18 − 9 = ☐
19 − 9 = ☐
20 − ☐ = 11

d
8 + 7 = ☐
15 − ☐ = 8
☐ − 8 = 7

Estimating and approximating

Learn

To estimate means to judge what the answer is, without calculating it exactly.
You can estimate the answer to an addition by first choosing how to round each number.

It is important to round in a way that makes the estimate easy to complete, but not in a way that is unhelpful.

Who has made the most useful estimate for the addition 756 + 489? Why?

I will round to the nearest 10 so I will use 760 + 480 to make my estimate.

I will round to the nearest 100 so I will use 800 + 500 to make my estimate.

Can you explain why rounding each number to the nearest 1 000 would not be helpful here?
Here are some more addition and subtraction calculations.
How will you round the numbers each time?

736 + 419 + 34   726 − 419   648 + 221 + 92   648 − 221 − 29

Practise

1 Choose whether you will round each number to the nearest 10 or the nearest 100. Use the rounded numbers to estimate the answer to each calculation. For each one, say if your estimate is **greater** or **smaller** than the actual answer.

a
542 + 378
542 + 328
625 + 143
675 + 143

b
367 + 79 + 236
367 + 71 + 236
367 + 79 + 286
327 + 71 + 286

c
782 + 873 + 267 + 554
782 + 873 + 222 + 554
715 + 873 + 222 + 554
715 + 823 + 222 + 514

d
562 − 378
542 − 328
625 − 183
655 − 143

e
367 − 79 − 136
367 − 39 − 186
367 + 79 − 236
367 − 79 + 236

f
982 − 323 − 247 − 144
982 + 323 − 247 + 144
982 − 323 + 247 − 144
982 − 323 + 247 + 144

Think like a mathematician

Think of subtraction calculations as the **difference** between two numbers on the number line. For example, 588 − 446:

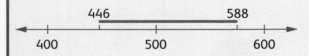

The gap between 446 and 500 is 64.
588 is 88 away from 500, and 64 + 88 > 100.
So, 588 − 446 > 100.

Try this

A teacher is hiring coaches to take these classes on an outing. Each coach takes 55 learners. How many coaches do they need altogether?

Class	Number of learners and their teachers
Class 1	31
Class 2	28
Class 3	32
Class 4	27
Class 5	29

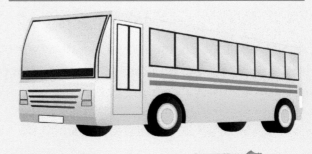

Choosing and using appropriate methods

Learn

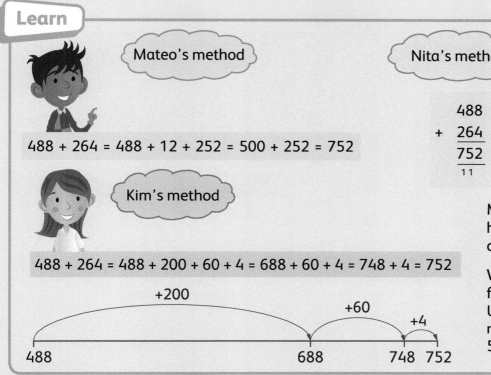

Mateo's method

488 + 264 = 488 + 12 + 252 = 500 + 252 = 752

Kim's method

488 + 264 = 488 + 200 + 60 + 4 = 688 + 60 + 4 = 748 + 4 = 752

Nita's method

$$\begin{array}{r} 488 \\ + \ 264 \\ \hline 752 \\ \hline {\scriptstyle 1\ 1} \end{array}$$

Mateo, Nita and Kim have different ways of calculating 488 + 264.

Will their methods work for any pair of numbers? Use two of these methods to calculate 594 + 378.

Practise

1 Add these numbers. Think about the method you will use each time.

a	b	c	d
34 + 14	26 + 18	64 + 53	72 + 48
534 + 14	326 + 18	764 + 53	672 + 48
534 + 214	326 + 418	764 + 253	672 + 548

e Use subtraction to check the last calculation in each box. Show the method you used each time.

2 Choose three cards to make a three-digit number.

Rearrange the three cards to make another three-digit number.

Use the two numbers to make an addition calculation.

4 5 2 6 3

a What is the largest total you can make with the three cards you have chosen?

b What is the smallest total you can make with the same three cards?

c Which three cards should you choose to make the highest possible total? What calculation did you use?

Adding lists of numbers

Learn

$$325 + 147 + 275$$

You have to add 325 and 147 first, and then add on 275.

It is easier to add 325 and 275 first and then add on 147.

You cannot do that. Kim! You will get a different answer.

What is the best way of adding 325 + 147 + 275? Why do you think it is the best way?

Practise

1 Add the three numbers in each circle. Then, add the numbers again, but do it in a different order. Which order was easier? Why?

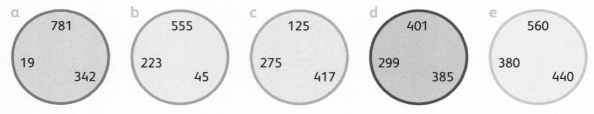

a
781
19
342

b
555
223
45

c
125
275
417

d
401
299
385

e
560
380
440

2 Choose a number from each bag, so that you have four numbers. Then, add your four numbers. Check your answer by adding the same four numbers in a different order. Repeat this five times, choosing a different set of four numbers each time.

125
49
350
330
642

275
30
720
331
884

398 51
280 242
321

402
70
650
243
442

Try this

If you add three three-digit numbers, the answer is 1 521. What could the numbers be?

Give at least three different answers.

Explaining methods

Learn

Caleb is adding 457 + 199 and Kim is calculating 457 – 199.

Caleb and Kim have both chosen to use the mental method of rounding and adjusting.

Why do you think they have chosen this method?

Have they both used the method correctly? Explain how you know.

I know that 457 + 200 is 657. I have added on one more than 199, so I have to take one away. The answer is 656.

I know that 457 – 200 is 257. I have taken away one more than 199, so I have to take one more away. The answer is 256.

+200
457   657

–200
257   457

Practise

1   Look at one box of calculations at a time.
    First choose the calculations in the box that you will solve using a mental method.
    Solve these and then complete the others using a written method.
    Move onto the next box.

a	b	c	d	e
465 + 235	567 + 895	400 – 198	889 + 111	798 – 349
487 + 669	399 + 567	894 – 576	846 – 432	513 – 365
783 – 299	485 + 879	432 + 608	902 – 452	500 – 251
600 + 382	500 – 275	298 + 302	350 + 351	668 – 479

2   a   Write an addition and subtraction calculation of your own that you will solve using a mental method.

    b   Now write another two calculations that you would solve using a written method.
        Explain your decisions.

Think like a mathematician

When you have to do a calculation, first think whether you can do it mentally.
Perhaps it is easier than it looks! You can rearrange the numbers or use another strategy. If you cannot do the calculation mentally, you could use a written method.

Solving problems

Learn

Look at the problem here. What calculations will you need to do?

At a concert, there were 299 men, 308 women, 192 boys and 349 girls. How many more adults were at the concert than children?

The problem can be represented using a bar model. What does the part labelled with the question mark represent?

Adults

299 men	308 women

192 boys	349 girls	

Children   ?

What strategies will you use to carry out the additions and subtraction? Why?

What is the answer to the problem?

At the concert, everyone was sitting down. There are 1 350 seats. How many seats were empty?

Practise

1 At the market, there were 249 men, 363 women and 51 boys. Altogether there were 703 people at the market.

   a How many girls were at the market?

   b How many more adults were at the market than children?

   c Which were there more of: men and boys or women and girls?

2 A bowl and six eggs weigh 900 g. The same bowl and four eggs weigh 700 g. How much does the bowl weigh?

3 Each column, row and diagonal add up to the same value if the numbers are added. Find the missing values for A, B, C and D.

A	273	234
156	B	39
C	D	312

Think like a mathematician

Think about the way that you can represent the problems to help you, perhaps using bars.

Self-check

A Place value and decimals

1 What do the highlighted digits represent in this number?
123 456.78

2 Put these numbers in increasing order, using the <, > or = signs.
Increasing order means going from smallest to largest.

117   17   0.17   17 000

3 Divide 7 000 by:
a 10
b 100
c 1 000

B Rounding and estimating

1 Round each number as shown.
a 6 087 to the nearest 1 000
b 64 850 to the nearest 100.

2 Use your rounding and estimating
skills to check which of these
calculations are correct and which
ones are not.
a 476 + 533 = 1 109
b 2 455 + 1 032 + 7 871 = 11 358
c 1 527 − 382 = 965
d 23 320 − 2 977 − 502 = 20 841
e 3 406 + 68 + 109 + 5 000 = 8 583

C Addition and subtraction

1 Do the following calculations. In each
case, choose whether to use a mental
method or a written method. For each
calculation, explain how you decided
what to do. If you choose a mental
method, explain what you did.
a 13 + 12 =
b 130 + 120 =
c 501 + 99 =
d 321 − 198 =
e 351 − 176 =
f 33 + 124 + 67 =
g 33 + 124 − 67 =

Unit 2 Measures and problem solving

⏻ 2a The metric system

Explore

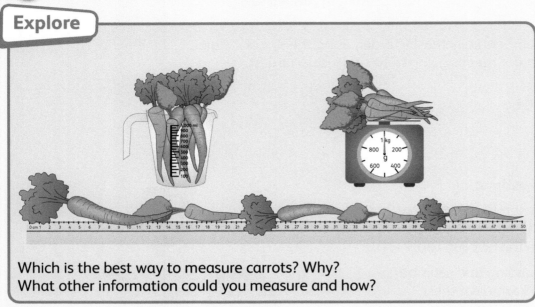

Which is the best way to measure carrots? Why?
What other information could you measure and how?

Reading and using decimal units

Learn

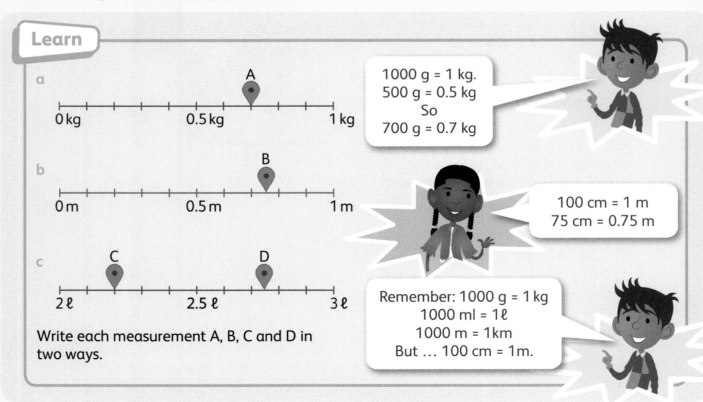

a   A

0 kg   0.5 kg   1 kg

1000 g = 1 kg.
500 g = 0.5 kg
So
700 g = 0.7 kg

b   B

0 m   0.5 m   1 m

100 cm = 1 m
75 cm = 0.75 m

c   C   D

2 ℓ   2.5 ℓ   3 ℓ

Write each measurement A, B, C and D in two ways.

Remember: 1000 g = 1 kg
1000 ml = 1ℓ
1000 m = 1km
But … 100 cm = 1m.

Practise

1   Write in grams and kilograms.

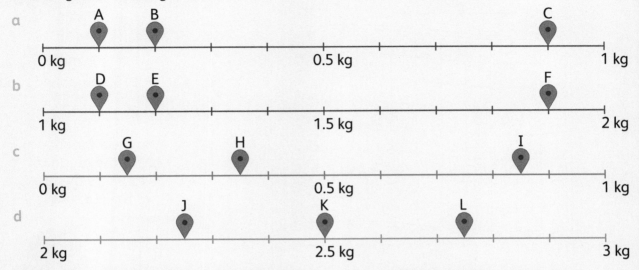

2   Mateo needs 0.72ℓ of liquid in each jug. How much liquid should he add to each jug?

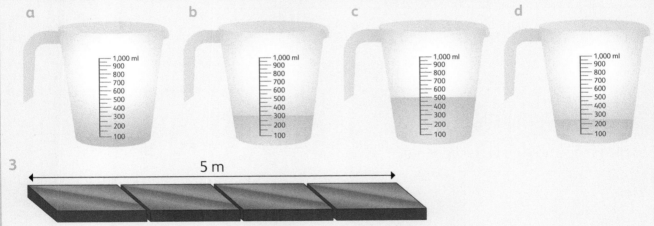

3

Mateo cuts this piece of wood into 4 equal lengths. How long is each piece?
Write your answer in m and cm.

Try this

Mateo has a jug containing
500 ml of water. He puts a stone
into the jug. He sees that the stone
sinks and that the water has risen
to 750 ml. What do you think he
has discovered about the stone?

Think like a mathematician

Water links weight, volume and length in the metric
system. A litre of pure water weighs one kilogram. One
millilitre of pure water fits into a one-centimetre cube.
1 ml of water fits perfectly into a 1 cm cube, if the
temperature is exactly 4°C. If the temperature is not
exactly 4°C, then the measure is approximate.

⏻ 2b Length, area and perimeter

Explore

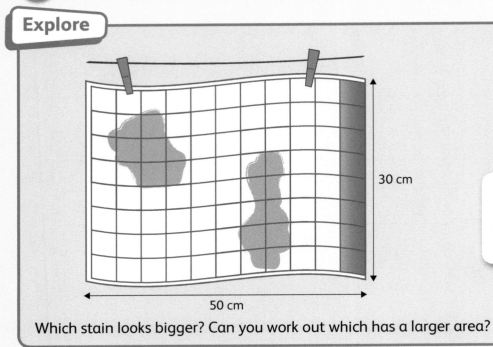

30 cm

50 cm

Which stain looks bigger? Can you work out which has a larger area?

Key words ⏻
area
perimeter
compound shape

Use the information about the tea towel to estimate the area of the tea towel.

Length, area and perimeter

Learn

Which shape has the largest area?

Which shape has the largest perimeter?

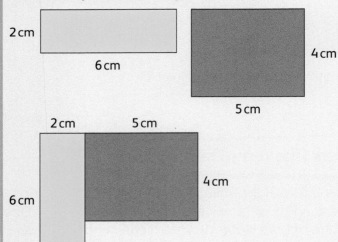

2 cm

6 cm

4 cm

5 cm

2 cm   5 cm

6 cm

4 cm

These shapes have been joined together to make a compound shape.

I can find the area of the third shape by adding the area of the yellow shape and the area of the red shape. To find the perimeter, I need to work out three more lengths.

Practise

1 Measure these rectangles to the nearest millimetre. Then calculate the area and perimeter for each. Write the area in mm².

a

b

c

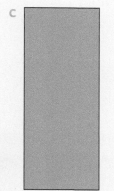

2 These diagrams show the rectangles from Question 1, but they have not been drawn to scale.

Draw them accurately using a ruler and grid paper.

Calculate the area and perimeter of each of these compound shapes:

a

b

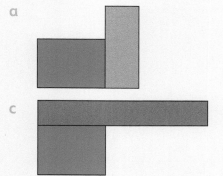

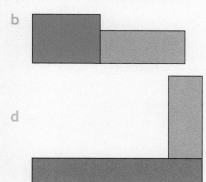

c

d

Try this

Here, three shapes have been joined together.

Make an estimate of the perimeter, then calculate to see if your estimate was close.

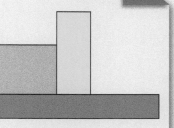

Use four shapes to create a compound shape that has a perimeter of approximately 50 cm.

Think like a mathematician

When measuring perimeter, it is easy to forget where you started. Put a pencil mark at the start point, or put your finger there to keep your place. That way you won't miss any sides!

2c Time

Explore

Key words

seconds
minutes
hours
day
year
century
decade
calendar

Getting the train

Arriving…

How long was the journey?

Is there more than one possible answer?
Give the answer in minutes.

What would you key into a calculator to work out the answer in seconds?

Telling the time and units of time

Learn

But what if it's p.m.?

My digital watch shows 24-hour time. Which clock does it match?

If it is 4.55 a.m., then in 12 hours a clock will say either
4.55 p.m., or 16.55 for the 24-hour time.
The digital watch would show 4.55 or 16.55.
Write digital times for the clocks in the morning and in the afternoon.

Practise

1 Write two digital times for each clock – one for morning and one for afternoon.

a	b	c	d	e	f

2 For each pair of times, say which duration is longer.

   a 32 seconds or 1 minute   b 30 hours or 1 day   c 100 days or 1 year

   d 13 years or 1 decade   e 99 years or 27 decades   f 800 years or 3 centuries

   g 50 hours or 2 days   h 7 weeks or 1 month   i 370 seconds or 1 hour

Try this

Today is Nita's tenth birthday.

Work out her age:

a in months   b in weeks   c in days.

Has Nita lived for a million minutes? How do you know?

Think like a mathematician

Remember:
- 60 seconds = one hour
- 60 minutes = one hour
- 365 days = one year
- 24 hours = one day
- 12 months = one year.

Calculating time intervals

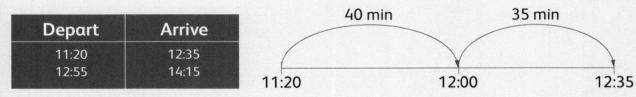

Depart	Arrive
11:20	12:35
12:55	14:15

40 minutes + 35 minutes = 75 minutes

The first journey takes 75 minutes or 1 hr 15 min.

Why is 75 minutes the same as 1 hour and 15 minutes?

Draw a number line to work out the next journey.

Practise

1   Each of these clocks shows the time in the morning. Write the time one and a half hours later using the 24-hour clock.

a    b

c

d    e    f

2 Draw a number line to calculate the length of time each journey takes.

	Depart	Arrive	Length of journey
A	09:30	10:15	
B	11:25	12:15	
C	11:55	13:05	
D	13:40	15:28	
E	19:49	22:11	
F	23:01	03:59	

3 A soccer game has two halves of 45 minutes each, separated by a 15-minute break at half-time.

  a How long is a soccer game in total? Answer in hours and minutes.

  b If a football game starts at 15:30, will it be finished by 6 p.m.?

  c If a football game is expected to finish at 20:55, when did it start?

  d If Nita plays in a soccer game that starts at 4 p.m., can she get a bus at 17:30 to travel home?

Try this

Depart	Arrive
11:30	12:00
17:45	18:15

I subtract the start time from the finish time:

$$18:15$$
$$-17:45$$
$$\overline{00:70}$$

So the journey took 70 minutes.

Explain the mistake that Mateo has made.

Find the correct answer by using a different method.

⟳ 2d Problem solving

Explore

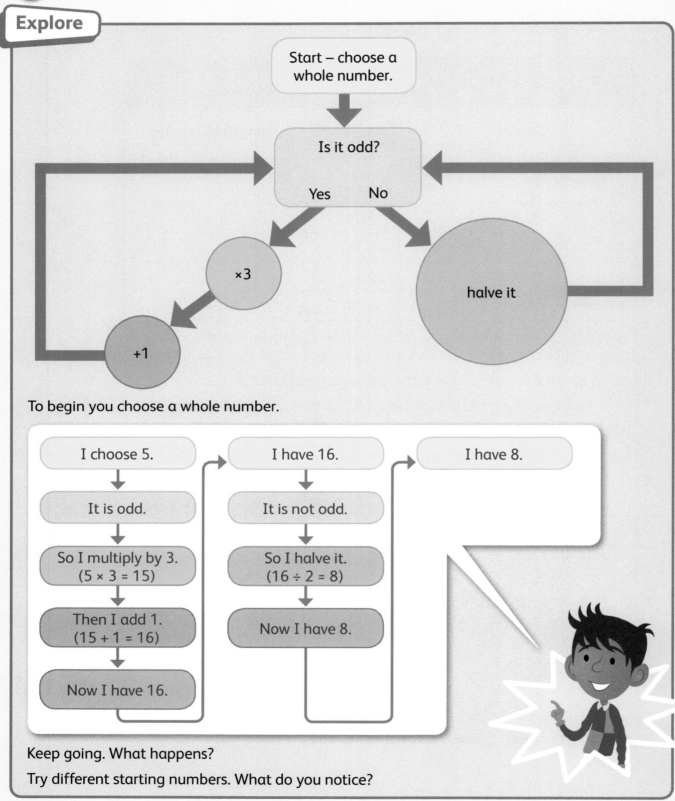

Start – choose a whole number.

Is it odd?

Yes   No

×3

halve it

+1

To begin you choose a whole number.

I choose 5.

It is odd.

So I multiply by 3.
(5 × 3 = 15)

Then I add 1.
(15 + 1 = 16)

Now I have 16.

I have 16.

It is not odd.

So I halve it.
(16 ÷ 2 = 8)

Now I have 8.

I have 8.

Keep going. What happens?

Try different starting numbers. What do you notice?

Solving problems

Mateo needs to paint this wall.

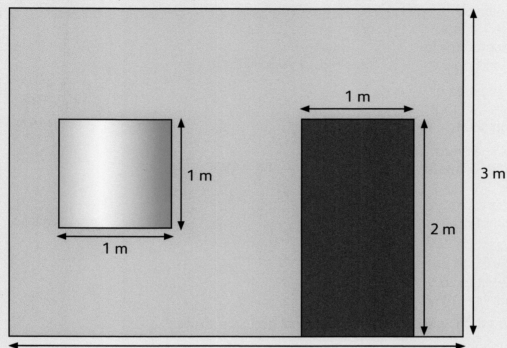

1 m

1 m

1 m

3 m

2 m

The door is
2 m high and
1 m wide.

The window
is 1 m × 1 m.

4 m

How much paint does he need to buy?
The wall is 3 m by 4 m.

He does not need to paint the door or the window.
The area of the door is 2 m × 1 m.
The area of the window is 1 m × 1 m.

He needs to paint the wall twice. This is called giving it two coats of paint.
Paint comes in tins that cover 3 m².

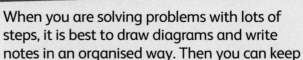

3 m squared

How many tins of paint should he buy?

Two coats of paint mean that Mateo has
to paint 9 m² × 2 = 18 m².

18 ÷ 3 = 6

Six tins would cover the walls exactly.
But he should buy one extra tin, to make
sure he has enough in case any paint
is spilled. Mateo decides to buy two extra
tins of paint.

Think like a mathematician

When you are solving problems with lots of
steps, it is best to draw diagrams and write
notes in an organised way. Then you can keep
track of which stage you are at, rather than
trying to keep track of everything in your head.

Practise

Thandi and her father are going to redecorate her bedroom. This means that they are going to repaint the walls, and fix a frieze along the top of each wall. A frieze is a decorated strip of wallpaper.

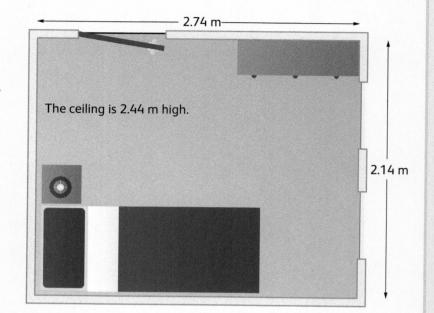

The ceiling is 2.44 m high.

2.74 m

2.14 m

1 They need to know the area of the walls to be painted, so that they can buy enough paint.

   a Use the sketch of the room to work out the approximate area of the walls. 'Approximate' means 'more or less' or an estimate.

   b Do you think your approximate answer will be greater than or less than a more accurate answer? Why?

   c What other information would you need for a more accurate answer?

   d Do you think your approximate answer is good enough for buying paint? Give your reasons.

2 Work out the perimeter of the ceiling. This is the length of frieze they should buy.

3 Thandi and her father will take a bus to go and buy the paint. Use the timetable to answer these questions about their journey.

Thandi's house	1	09:30	09:48	10:01	10:16	10:33	10:45	11:01	11:10
Paint shop	2	09:42	10:00	10:13	10:28	10:45	10:57	11:13	11:22

Paint shop	34	10:19	10:34	10:49	11:04	11:19	11:34	11:49	12:04
Thandi's house	15	10:31	10:46	11:01	11:16	11:31	11:46	12:01	12:16

   a How many buses go to the paint shop between 10:00 and 11:00?

   b How long does the bus journey to the paint shop take?

   c If they get to the bus stop at 10:00, when should they be at the paint shop?

   d If they then take one hour to buy paint, what is the next bus they can catch home?

   e When will that bus arrive at their stop?

4 When Thandi and her father get to the paint shop, they look at the instructions on the cans of paint that they like. Five litres of paint will cover 35 m². They will need to give the walls two coats (layers) of paint. The shop sells the paint in these sizes:

● One litre costs $14.99.

● 2.5 litres costs $29.99.

● Five litres costs $49.00.

a How many litres of paint do they need? Remember that they have to paint everything twice, because they need to paint two coats of paint.

b What is the cheapest way of buying the amount of paint that they need.

5 Plan the day's painting job by putting these tasks in the right order. Be sure to include any times at which Thandi and her father can't work. If they start at 09:00 today, when will they finish the job?

Here are the tasks that Thandi and her father need to do. These tasks are not shown in the right order.

• Fix the frieze – 30 mins

• Paint the walls with the second coat of paint – 3 hours

• Move the furniture out (or back in again) – 30 mins

• Paint the walls with the first coat of paint – 3 hours

• Allow the paint to dry – 5 hours

Self-check

A The metric system

1 There are no units shown in these pictures. Give the correct unit of measure for each situation.

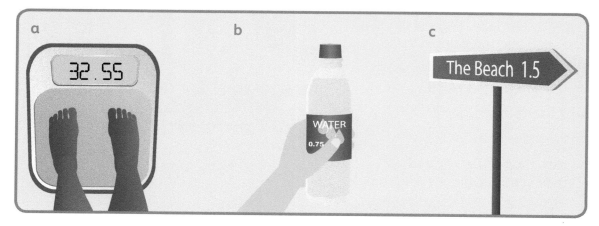

B Length, area and perimeter

1 Look at the shape below.

a Calculate the area and perimeter of this squared piece of paper.
b Estimate the area of the picture of the rabbit.
c Say or show how your answers were worked out.

C Time

1 How long is 100 minutes in hours?

2 A concert starts at six thirty p.m. and ends at 21:45. How long is the concert?

3 Nita does 45 minutes of homework, starting at 05:30. When will she complete the homework?

4 On 1st September Mateo starts making a model. He thinks it will take 22 hours to make. If he works for one hour a day, on which day will he finish?

⏻ 3a Factors and multiples

Explore

**Party Box of
12 Doughnuts**
the most
shareable number

Key words ⏻
factor
multiply
factor pair
common factor
multiple
even
common multiple
prime number

Why does the box say that 12 is 'the most shareable number'?

Finding factors of numbers

Learn

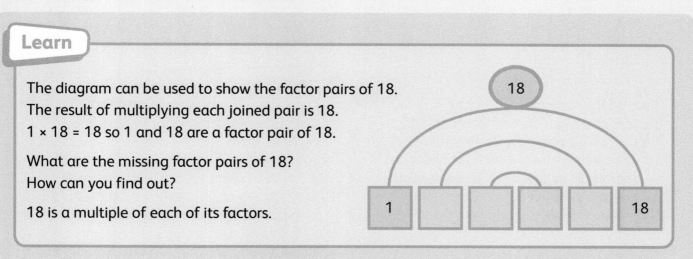

The diagram can be used to show the factor pairs of 18.
The result of multiplying each joined pair is 18.
1 × 18 = 18 so 1 and 18 are a factor pair of 18.

What are the missing factor pairs of 18?
How can you find out?

18 is a multiple of each of its factors.

18

| 1 | | | | | 18 |

Practise

1 Are these statements true or false?

Write a fact each time to prove your thinking.

The first one has been done for you.

a 9 is not a factor of 50.   True. 9 × 5 = 45 and 9 × 6 = 54. 50 is not in the 9× table.

b 2 is a factor of 27.

c 10 is a factor of 100.

d 72 is a factor of 8.

e 8 is a factor of 72.

f 6 and 7 are a factor pair of 42.

g 6 and 21 are factors of 42.

h 6 and 21 are a factor pair of 42.

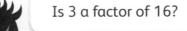

Is 3 a factor of 16?

3 × 5 = 15 and 3 × 6 = 18. So 3 is not a factor of 16.

2 Find all the factor pairs of these numbers.
Show your answers using factor pair diagrams.

a 21   b 42

c 36   d 84

e Why is 2 a factor of 42, but not a factor of 21?

3 Find all the numbers that are:

a factors of 24

b common factors of 24 and 36 (that is, they must be factors of both 24 and 36)

c common factors of 21 and 42.

Try this

Find all the factors of 10, all the factors of 20, and all the factors of 30. Say which numbers are common factors of all three numbers. Which numbers are not common factors of all three numbers? What do you notice?

Think like a mathematician

When you are looking for factors of a number, think about some facts you already know to help you:
- All even numbers are multiples of two
- Multiples of six must be multiples of three, because there are two groups of three in a group of six.

What do you know about other multiples?

Multiples

Learn

| 25 | 40 | 36 | 72 | 30 | 90 | 28 | 45 | 20 | 75 | 54 | 15 |

Here are some multiples of three different numbers.

What do you notice about the numbers in the circles?

What do you notice about the numbers in the pentagons?

How about the numbers in the squares?

The numbers in the squares are all multiples of 10, but they are also multiples of 2 and 5.

Multiples of 10 are common multiples of 2 and 5 because they can be found in the multiplication tables for both 2 and 5.

Practise

1 Say whether these numbers are multiples of 2, 3, or 4, or a combination of these numbers, or none of these numbers.

   a 15   b 18   c 8   d 38

   e 17   f 21   g 24   h 30

2 Write out these multiples and say which patterns you see in your answers.

   a The multiples of 10 up to 120   b The multiples of 25 up to 250

   c The multiples of 50 up to 500   d The multiples of 100 up to 1 000

3 Find all the common multiples of 4 and 5 up to 60.

   What do you notice?

Try this

Find the common multiples of 4, 6 and 8, up to 100. What patterns do you see?

How can you explain the pattern?

Think like a mathematician

You can always multiply the two numbers together to find one common multiple. However, this may not be the <u>lowest</u> common multiple. For example, 3 × 6 = 18. So, 18 is one common multiple of 3 and 6. However, 6 and 12 are other common multiples and are lower than 18.

Prime numbers

Learn

What do you notice about these factor pair diagrams?

7		13		17		23
1	7	1	13	1	17	1	23

I've spotted a pattern: 7, 13, 17, 23. I think that 27 must also be prime because it comes next in the pattern. Do you agree?

Some numbers have exactly two factors: one and the number itself. Numbers like this are called prime numbers. Prime numbers have exactly two arrays.

Here are the two arrays for the prime number 7.

Use an array to explain why the number 1 is not a prime number.

1×7

7×1

Practise

1   Which of these numbers is definitely not a prime number? Explain how you know.

44	19	2	11	35	100

2   Mateo wants to place these numbers on a Venn diagram.

15	9	5	2	53	29	1	36	49	81

Should he place each number in section A, B, C or D?

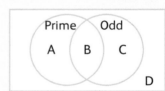

Try this

Eratosthenes, an Ancient Greek mathematician, invented a way of finding prime numbers. It is called the 'sieve of Eratosthenes'.
Nita has started to use this test to find prime numbers. Here is part of the 100 square she is using to help her.

1	2	3	4	5	6	7	8	9	10
11	12	13	14	15	16	17	18	19	20
21	22	23	24	25	26	27	28	29	30

She starts by crossing out 1 as it is not a prime number. She circles the next number, 2, but crosses out all other multiples of 2. Next she circles the number, 3, but crosses out all other multiples of 3 left on the 100 square. Why does she circle 5 next and miss out 4?

Use a 100 square to find all the prime numbers up to 100.

3b Number patterns, sequences and generalisations

I think that 116 will come next.

26, 51, 76, 101

Key words

generalisation
sequence
term
rule
odd

What patterns do you notice in this number sequence?

How can you explain the mistake that Kim has made?

Number sequences

Learn

You can look for patterns that you recognise to help find the rule.

What pattern do you recognise in the sequence 250, 200, 150, 100, 50?

How about the sequence 2, 4, 8, 16, 32?

What is the next term in each of these sequences?

You can also look at the differences between the numbers in the sequence.

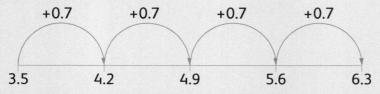

+0.7   +0.7   +0.7   +0.7

3.5   4.2   4.9   5.6   6.3

The rule for the sequence 3.5, 4.2, 4.9, 5.6, 6.3 is add 0.7.

A sequence has numbers that are written in a particular order. We also call these numbers 'terms'. The terms in a sequence follow a rule.

1 What are the missing terms in these sequences?

Write the rule each time.

a _____ , 210 , 280 , 350, _____

b 1 500, 2 200, _____ , _____ , 4 300

c 2, 1.7, _____ , _____ , 0.8 , _____

d −12, _____ , 0 , 6, 12, _____

e 120, 60, 30 , _____ , _____

2 Here is a sequence of circles.

What is true or false about this sequence of circles?

a Each term contains only an even number of circles.

b The number of circles in each term get larger by the same amount each time.

c The sequence rule cannot be that you double the number of circles each time.

d The fourth term has three more circles than the third term.

What is the rule? Can you sketch the next term?

Generalisations about odd and even numbers

An even number can be shown in an array with two matching rows.
An odd number cannot.

Which even numbers and odd numbers are represented here?

Look at what happens when you add pairs of odd and even numbers.

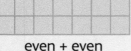 

even + even   even + odd   odd+ odd

Can you explain what will happen when another odd number is added each time?

For example: even + even + odd?

You can explore subtraction in a similar way. Think about 10 − 4.

The array shows the difference between the even numbers 10 and 4.

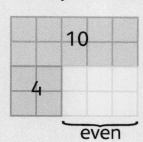

10

4

even

This array shows that the difference between these two even numbers is even.

You can say that even − even = even.

Is this always true?

Practise

1 Choose numbers and sketch arrays to prove whether the following statements are true or false:

   a even − odd = odd   b odd − odd = odd

   c odd + even = odd   d odd + odd + even = even

   e odd + even + odd + even = odd

2 Are the answers to these calculations even numbers or odd numbers? You do not need to work out the answers.

a		b		c	
64 + 22 =		90 − 31 =		90 + 31 + 22	
23 + 64 =		91 − 30 =		190 + 310 + 221	
22 + 65 =		91 − 31 =		90 − 22 + 31	

Think like a mathematician

Remember that addition can be carried out in any order, so it doesn't matter if the calculation is odd + even or even + odd. The result will be the same.

⏻ 3c **Multiplication and division**

Key words
divide
remainder

Explore

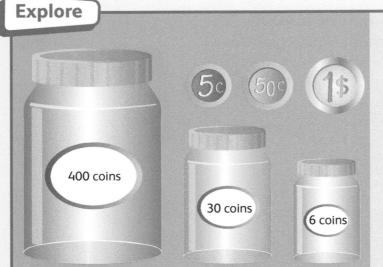

One of the jars holds only 5c coins.
Another holds only 50c coins.
The other holds only $1 coins (100 c).

How much money could be in each jar?
What is the largest total of the three jars?
What is the smallest total of the three jars?

Multiplying multiples of ten

Learn

The calculation 30 × 40 can be rewritten using factors.
You can use place value to help multiply by 10 so it is useful to find a factor pair for each number where one factor is 10.

3 and 10 is a factor pair for 30.

4 and 10 is a factor pair for 40.

So 30 × 40 can we written as 3 × 10 × 4 × 10 and reordered as 3 × 4 × 10 × 10.

The calculation is represented here using arrays.
What part of the calculation does each array show?
What will the missing array look like and what calculation will it represent?

30 × 40 = 1 200.

How can we use this method to solve 30 × 400?
Which factor pairs will you choose this time?

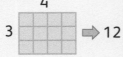

Practise

1 Use factors to help complete these calculations mentally.

Write the factors you use each time.

a 10 × 20 = ☐   b 30 × 10 = ☐   c 50 × 100 = ☐

d 30 × 20 = ☐   e 20 × 40 = ☐   f 30 × 300 = ☐

2 Find the missing numbers to make these calculations correct.

a 30 × ☐ = 1 200   b ☐ × 40 = 12 000

c 60 × 30 = ☐   d 30 × ☐ = 18 000

e ☐ × 300 = 1 800   f 20 × ☐ = 1 600

g ☐ × 800 = 16 000   h 20 × ☐ = 16 000

3 The water in this container fills 60 cups. Each cup holds 400 ml.

How many 300 ml glasses can be filled with the same amount of water?

4 A factory makes bars of soap that weigh 100 grams each.
The soap is packed into boxes, which each contain 30 bars of soap.
A lorry is loaded with 200 boxes.

a How much does a box of soap weigh?

b How many bars of soap are on the lorry?

c How much does all the soap on the lorry weigh?

water

Try this

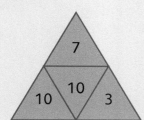

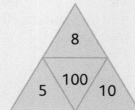

The four numbers in each triangle are the factors that have been used to help multiply two numbers.

☐ × ☐ =

What calculation could each triangle represent?

There is more than one solution for each triangle.

Multiplying near multiples of 10

Learn

Multiplying a number by 10 can be solved mentally using knowledge of place value.

Rounding to a multiple of 10 and adjusting is a useful method to multiply a near multiple of 10.

Look at the calculation 12 × 19.

19 is a near multiple of 10 as it is one less than 20.

So you can find 12 × 20 and then subtract 12 × 1.

The arrays help make sense of the method.

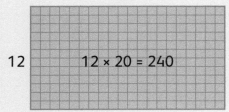

The calculation 12 × 19 is broken into two parts as (12 × 20) − (12 × 1).

Can you explain the method and sketch the arrays to help calculate 12 × 21?

Think like a mathematician

Remember to use what you know about multiplying by multiples of 10 to help you. Fo example 12 × 30 as 12 × 3 × 10

Practise

1 Use the rounding and adjusting method to help multiply by near multiples of 10.

Sketch any arrays you need to help you.

a 8 × 19   b 8 × 21

c 12 × 29   d 12 × 31

e 15 × 19   f 21 × 15

g 8 × 99   h 8 × 101

2 Now try these calculations. Think carefully about how you need to adjust your answer each time.

a 12 × 18

b 12 × 22

c 15 × 28

d 15 × 32

e 8 × 98

f 8 × 102

3 Mateo makes a line of 17 sticks that are each 31 cm long. Nita makes a line of 35 sticks that are each 22 cm long. Whose line is longer, and by how much?

Try this

Mateo and Nita use the rounding and adjusting method to help multiply two numbers.

Mateo calculates 7 × 20 and then adds 14 to his answer.

What is his calculation and the final answer?

Nita also calculates 7 × 20, but she subtracts 14 from her answer.

What is her calculation and final answer?

Using doubling and halving as a strategy for multiplication

Learn

All numbers can be represented using arrays. The number of rows and columns in an array show the factors of the number.

Look at these arrays and the matching multiplication facts for the number 20.

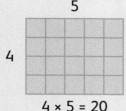

4 × 5 = 20

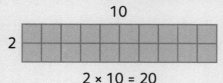

2 × 10 = 20

1 × 20 = 20

The 2 × 10 array has the same total number of squares as the 4 × 5 array, but it is arranged a little differently. It has half the number of rows and double the number of columns.

Now look at the array for 2 × 10 and then for 1 × 20.

What do you notice about the number of rows and columns this time?

So, 4 × 5 = 2 × 10 = 1 × 20. 1 × 20 is an easy calculation.

Knowing that you can halve one number and double the other in a multiplication calculation and still end up with the same answer (product) is a useful mental strategy.

Practise

1 Use the doubling and halving strategy to solve these multiplications. Remember to think about which number you will halve.

a 8 × 22 b 24 × 4 c 5 × 38 d 35 × 16

2 These rectangles all have the same area. Do you agree? Explain how you know.

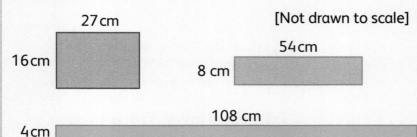

[Not drawn to scale]

Think like a mathematician

When there are two even numbers in the multiplication calculation, think about:
- which one will allow you to keep halving and still result in an even number

or

- which one will need to be halved fewer times to reach an easier calculation.

Multiplying larger numbers

Learn

Here are three representations for the calculation 7 × 2 465.

What is the same and what is different about them?

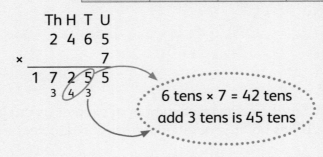

	2 000 +	400 +	60 +	5	
7	14 000	2 800	420	35	= 17 255

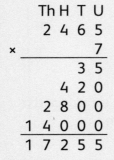

```
  Th H T U
   2 4 6 5
×        7
─────────
       3 5
     4 2 0
   2 8 0 0
 1 4 0 0 0
─────────
 1 7 2 5 5
```

```
  Th H T U
   2 4 6 5
×        7
─────────
 1 7 2 5 5
   3 4 3
```

6 tens × 7 = 42 tens
add 3 tens is 45 tens

Now think about the calculation 7 × 2 500.

Why do you think that a mental method would be best here?

Practise

1 Solve these calculations. Will you solve them using a written method or a mental method?

　a 267 × 8　　　　　b 3 067 × 9　　　　　c 7 000 × 5

　d 2 800 × 4　　　　　e 4 783 × 7　　　　　f 3 200 × 3

2 Each person in a team of 8 people runs 2 575 m.
　Each person in a team of 6 people runs 3 475 m.

　Which team runs the furthest in total?

　How much further does the whole team run?

3 Which rectangle has the largest area?

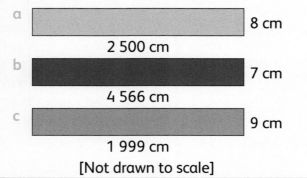

　a　　　　　　　　　　　　　　　8 cm
　　　　2 500 cm

　b　　　　　　　　　　　　　　　7 cm
　　　　4 566 cm

　c　　　　　　　　　　　　　　　9 cm
　　　　1 999 cm

　[Not drawn to scale]

Think like a mathematician

Remember to decide whether you will need a written method or mental method to complete each calculation. Multiplication facts and place value will help you here.

Dividing two-digit numbers by a single digit

Learn

What do the orange arrays tell you about the numbers 28 and 32?

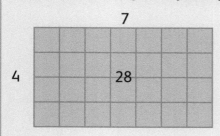
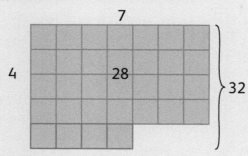

Notice how the number 32 is partitioned into 28 and 4.
How does this help with the calculation 32 ÷ 7?

You can use the array to prove that $32 \div 7 = 4 \, r \, 4$ or $4\frac{4}{7}$

What do you need to do with the remainder in the problems below?

32 children arrange themselves in groups of seven.

a How many groups of seven can be made? How many children will be left without a group?

b What fraction of a whole group do the remaining children represent?

Practise

1 Sketch an array for each of these division calculations. Turn any remainders into fractions.

  a 56 ÷ 7   b 58 ÷ 7   c 81 ÷ 9   d 85 ÷ 9   e 108 ÷ 9   f 111 ÷ 9

2 Complete these calculations mentally using your multiplication facts to help you.

  a 23 ÷ 2   b 13 ÷ 3   c 71 ÷ 7   d 37 ÷ 9   e 77 ÷ 6   f 59 ÷ 8

3 Five identical boxes weigh 48 kg. What is the mass of one box?

4 Nita has seventeen pencils.

  a If she shares them with four other children, how many does each child get? Are there any left over?

  b Are there any number of children who can share 17 pencils exactly, with no remainder? Why?

Think like a mathematician

Don't forget to simplify any fractions in your answers to their lowest terms, for example $\frac{1}{3}$, not $\frac{3}{9}$.

Solving problems

Look at this problem. What is the problem asking you to do?

> A clumsy shop assistant knocks over 12 bottles of sauce. Each bottle contains 75 ml of sauce. They all break. His boss is so shocked by the noise that she drops and breaks a litre bottle of milk.
>
> Which accident made the bigger puddle?

The amount of sauce can be found by multiplying 75×12.

Which strategy will you use to complete this calculation? Why?

The sauce puddle is 900 ml.

Which is more, 900 ml of sauce or 1 litre of milk? How much more?

Practise

1   Pencils cost 24 cents each. What will it cost to buy pencils for a class of 30 children?

2   Which has the larger area: a board measuring 39 cm × 41 cm or a board measuring 25 cm × 84 cm?

3   Caleb is learning karate. He will practise for two 45-minute sessions a week.

   a   Will he have practised for more than 50 hours after one year of practicing?

   b   How many hours of practice will he have done after one year?

4   A party of 30 people are going on a trip. They hire 9-seater minibuses to take them. They also hire <u>one</u> 4-seater small car. How many minibuses did they hire?

5   Each shape represents a number. What is the value of each shape?

a   ← total 240

     total 132

b   ← total 240

     total 180

I am thinking of a two-digit number. If I divide it by 7, there is a remainder of 3. If I divide it by 9, there is a remainder of 7.

Which number is Nita thinking of?

Self-check

A Factors and multiples

1 Find all the factors of 48.

2 Are there any even numbers that are prime numbers? Explain your answer.

3 Find the common multiples of 2 and 3 up to 20.

B Number patterns, sequences and generalisations

1 Find the next two terms in this sequence. What rule generates the sequence?

   3, 6, 12, 24, 48…

2 How many squares will be in the 8th term in this sequence?
   How many squares will be in the 10th term?

   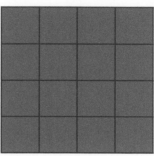

3 Are these statements true or false?

   a Even + even = even   b Odd − even = even

   c Even − odd = odd   d Odd + odd = even

C Multiplication and division

1 Answer these questions.

   a 400 × 20 = ☐   b 60 × 30 = ☐   c ☐ × 50 = 4 500

2 Write the digit 3, 4 or 7 each time to make these calculations correct.

   a 84 ÷ 9 = 9 r ☐   b 55 ÷ ☐ = 7 r 6

   c 55 ÷ 8 = 6 r ☐   d 96 ÷ ☐ = 24

3 Complete these calculations. Think carefully about the method you will use each time.

   a 91 × 7 = ☐   b 15 × 24 = ☐   c 8 × 57 = ☐

   d 472 × 8 = ☐   e 47 × 19 = ☐   f 2759 × 3 = ☐

Unit 4 Geometry and problem solving

4a Classifying 2-D shapes

Explore

Two identical squares have been made from coloured tissue paper.

They make a new shape when overlapped.

Here the overlap makes a triangle. What properties does the overlap triangle have?

Key words

polygon
quadrilateral
rectangle
parallel
square
parallelogram
rhombus
trapezium

Can you make a quadrilateral with no equal angles?

What other shapes can you make by overlapping two squares?

Use words such as: angle, polygon, quadrilateral, obtuse, acute.

Try this

How many squares are there in this picture of a polygon rabbit? Take care, they are not all easy to see!

Polygons

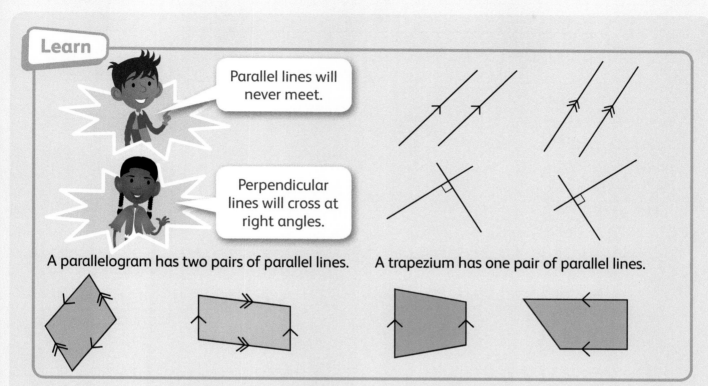

Parallel lines will never meet.

Perpendicular lines will cross at right angles.

A parallelogram has two pairs of parallel lines.

A trapezium has one pair of parallel lines.

Practise

1 Use squared or dotty paper. Draw three different parallelograms and three different trapeziums. Draw the marks to show pairs of parallel lines.

2 One fold has turned a rectangle into a trapezium.

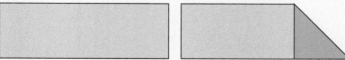

Investigate how many different polygons you can fold from a single rectangle.

a Three different trapeziums

b Two different parallelograms

c A kite

d A pentagon with a pair of parallel sides and a pair of perpendicular sides.

Try this

Make a 10 cm by 10 cm square from squared paper.
By folding, can you make two different hexagons that have three pairs of parallel lines?
Try to make an octagon with no pairs of parallel lines.

4b 3-D and 2-D shapes

Explore

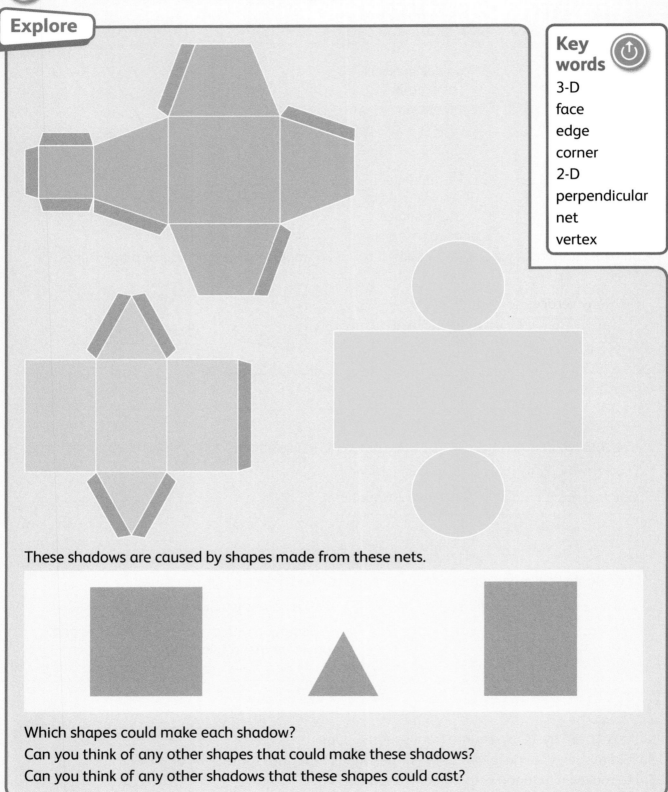

Key words
3-D
face
edge
corner
2-D
perpendicular
net
vertex

These shadows are caused by shapes made from these nets.

Which shapes could make each shadow?

Can you think of any other shapes that could make these shadows?

Can you think of any other shadows that these shapes could cast?

3-D and 2-D shapes

Learn

Mateo has made a shape from red cubes.

Nita has drawn 3 shapes on the paper. Which matches Mateo's shape?

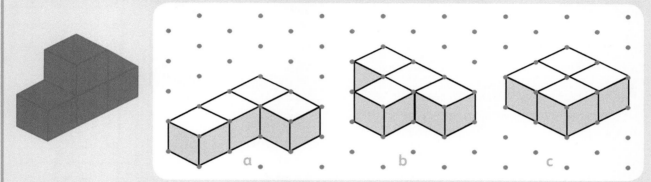

a   b   c

How many vertices, faces and edges does each 3-D shape have?

Practise

1   Match each shape to its drawing.

a   b   c   d   e

1

2

3

4

5

2   Record how many vertices, faces and edges each shape has.

4c Angles in a triangle

Key words
protractor
angle
internal
triangle

Explore

I noticed that when I put all the corners together, they fit perfectly along the edge of the table.

Measuring angles in a triangle

Learn

How to use a protractor to measure an angle.

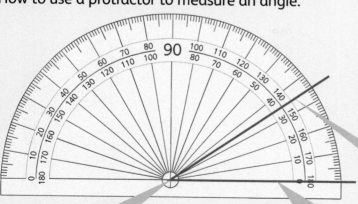

We use a **protractor** to measure **angles**. We measure angles in degrees. We write degrees in this way: 35 degrees = 35°.

3. Read off the size of the angle.

2. Position the protractor crosshairs exactly at the angle.

1. Choose a baseline to measure from.

Practise

1   Mateo has measured the angles carefully. Find the sum of all three angles for each triangle.
    What do you notice?

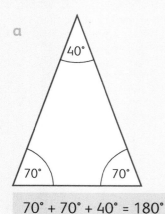

a

70° + 70° + 40° = 180°

b

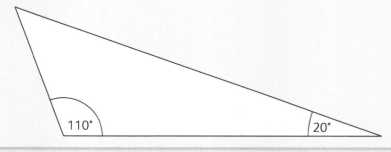

c

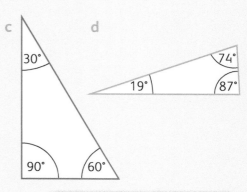

d

My sister told me that all the internal angles of a triangle always add up to 180 degrees.

2   Nita measured two angles of this triangle.
    Calculate what the last angle should be, and then measure to check.

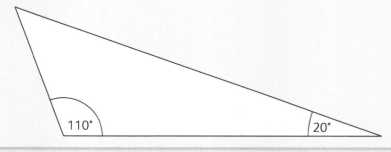

110°   20°

Try this

Check Nita's conjecture above in the *Practise* activity.

Draw five different triangles. Then measure the angles as accurately as you can.

They should each sum to 180 degrees.

Think like a mathematician

The internal angles of a shape are the angles at each corner, on the inside. The external angle is the angle through which you would turn if you are walking around the perimeter of the polygon.

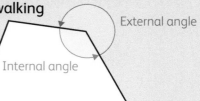

External angle

Internal angle

4d Working with coordinates

Explore

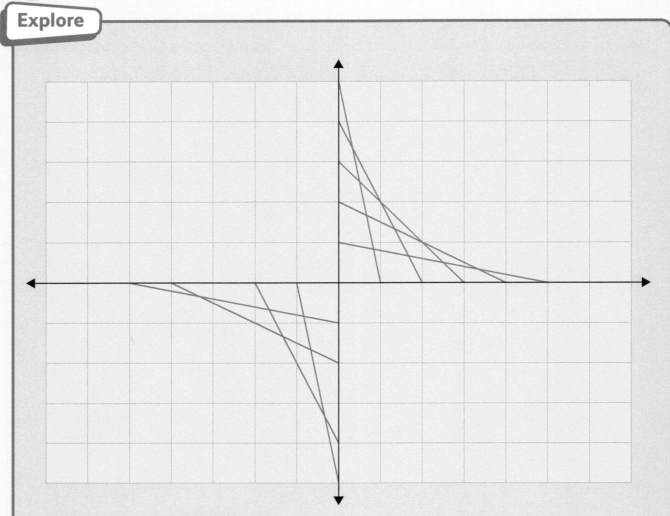

Nita has drawn part of a pattern.

Describe how this pattern is made.

One line has been missed. Can you describe where the line should be drawn without pointing at the grid?

Explain how you think the pattern would continue in the rest of the grid.

Key words

quadrant

x-axis

y-axis

coordinates

Coordinates in four quadrants

Learn

You can plot points that just use positive numbers, like point A (5, 3). If you extend the **x-axis** and **y-axis** beyond zero, you can also plot points that have negative coordinates. What are the **coordinates** of B, C and D?

Point B is at x = 2 and y = −3. Its coordinates are (2, −3).

Point C is at x = −3 and y = −5. Its coordinates are (−3, −5).

Point D is at x = −1 and y = 1. Its coordinates are (−1, 1).

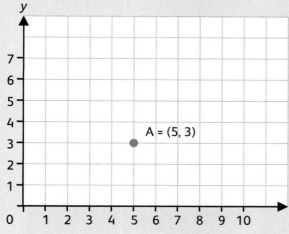

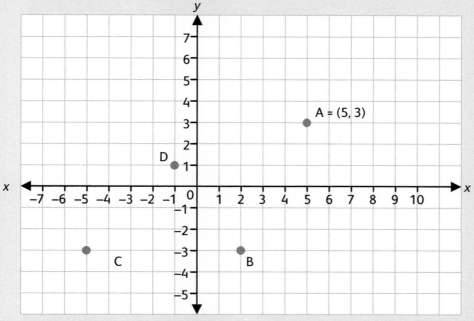

Practise

1 a What are the coordinates of
   the points A, B, C and D on
   this graph?

   b A, B and C form three corners
   of a rectangle. Write the
   coordinates of the fourth
   corner.

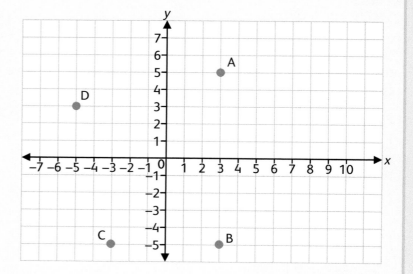

2 Write the coordinates of points
  a, b, c and d.

3 The blue dots and the red dots
  each lie on a straight line.

   a Write the coordinates of
   another three blue dots
   and another three red dots
   in the pattern.

   b Decide if a, b, c or d would be
   on either of the lines.

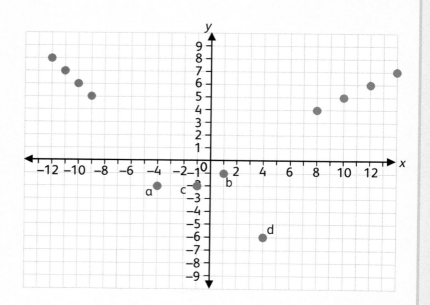

Try this

Draw your own coordinate grid from
−5 to 5 on the x- and y-axes. Plot the
points for a rectangle, a pentagon,
and a parallelogram. Record the
coordinates accurately.

Think like a mathematician

The x-coordinate is always given first.
Remember: Go along first, then up.

 4e Transformations

Explore

Tetrominoes are shapes made by joining four squares along an edge.

A tetromino is the same as another tetromino if it can be rotated and/or reflected to look the same.

Pentominoes are made by joining five squares along their edges.

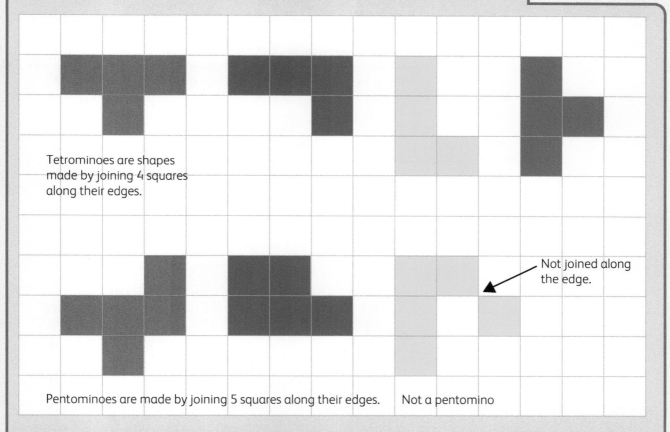

Tetrominoes are shapes made by joining 4 squares along their edges.

Pentominoes are made by joining 5 squares along their edges.

Not joined along the edge.

Not a pentomino

There are two different tetrominoes here.

Which two are the same shape rotated?

In total, there are seven different tetrominoes and 12 different pentominoes. Can you make or draw them all?

Translation on a coordinate grid

Learn

A translation is where a shape slides into a new position without rotating or reflecting.

The blue tetromino has been translated ten squares left and two squares up.

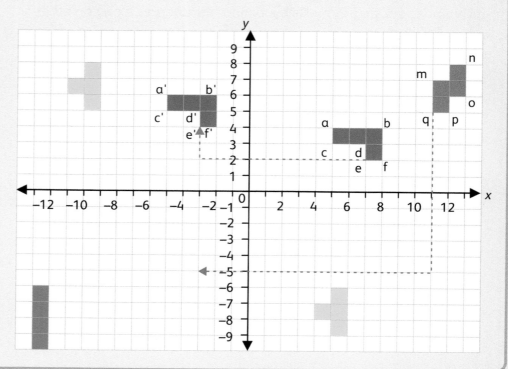

Practise

Use the *Learn* panel to answer these questions.

1 a Describe the translation shown for the red tetromino.

   b Write the new coordinates for points m, n, o, p and q after the translation has happened.

2 Describe two different translations to move a yellow tetromino to the position of the other.

3 The green shape is repeatedly translated two right, one up. Write the coordinates for all four corners after ten of these translations.

Try this

What would be the coordinates of the green shape after 25 translations of one right, one up? What about 100?

Think like a mathematician

When a point has been translated, use an apostrophe to show the new point. For example, point b is named b' after a translation.

Rotation about a point

Learn

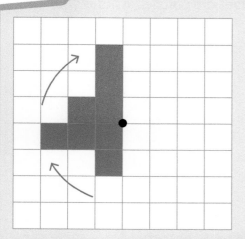

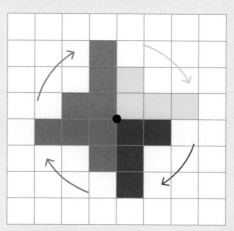

A rotation around a vertex moves the shape as if you spin it while pinning the vertex in place.

Look at this pattern which is created by repeated clockwise rotations through 90 degrees.

Do you think the pattern would be the same if you rotated around a different vertex?

Practise

1 Make your own rotation patterns by rotating these tetrominoes around the vertex marked.

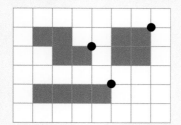

2 Investigate what happens when you rotate the same shape from a different vertex.

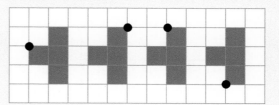

Try this

Create your own rotation challenge by rotating shapes made from squares and half squares around a vertex.

Here is one example, but you could create your own:

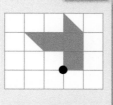

Think like a mathematician

Leave enough room to allow for the rotating patterns. It may help to make the shape from cubes or cut it out from paper so that you can test the rotations.

Self-check

A Classifying 2-D shapes

1 Draw a shape that has four sides, and both pairs of sides are parallel. What is your shape called?

2 Name at least three types of quadrilaterals that are not squares.

B 3-D and 2-D shapes

1 What 3-D shape would this net fold into?

2 Which of these properties would the 3-D shape have?
   a Rectangular faces
   b A pair of parallel faces
   c Some perpendicular faces
   d Some perpendicular edges

C Angles in a triangle

1 Measure the internal angles of this triangle, and then add them up.

D Working with coordinates

Look at rectangle ABCD.

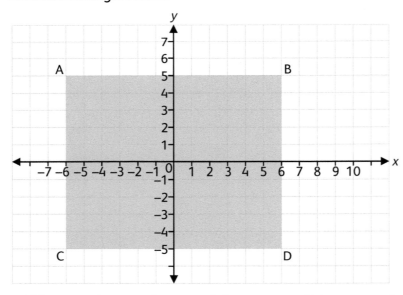

1 What are the coordinates of the corners of the rectangle ABCD?

2 Which of these points are inside ABCD?
   a (0, 0)   b (6, 6)
   c (3, −2)   d (−5, −4)
   e (−6, 6)

E Transformations

Look at this graph and then answer the questions.

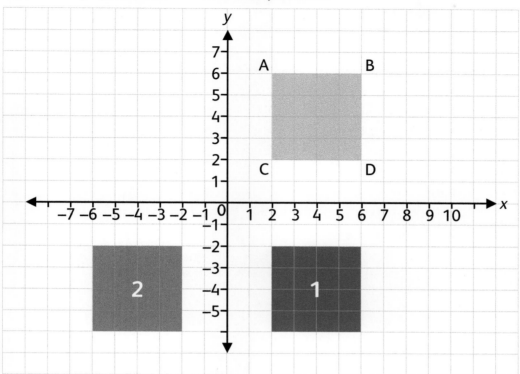

1 Describe two different transformations that would move square ABCD to cover square 1.

2 Describe two different transformations that would move square ABCD to cover square 2.

Unit 5 Problem solving and review

5a Problem solving

Challenge 1

Li, Kim, Mateo, Thandi and Nita stay at the Riverside hotel while on a school debating trip.

The Riverside Hotel has 66 rooms. Floor 1 has Rooms 1 to 22. Floor 2 has rooms 23 to 44 and Floor 3 has rooms 45 to 66.

Room numbers that are divisible by three have a view over the water. The others face the forest.

Use the following clues to answer the questions.

THE RIVERSIDE HOTEL

Clues

- Thandi and Kim have rooms with a view over the water. Mateo, Li and Nita have rooms that look out over the forest.

- Li has the highest room number on the first floor.

- Kim and Nita are the only learners staying on the second floor.

- Thandi's room number is double Kim's room number.

- All the learners' room numbers add up to 220.

a Who is staying in Room 44?

b Work out the relationship between the room number and the name of the learner staying in it. (Hint: think about how many letters there are in each learner's name.)

Challenge 2

This is the logo of the Riverside Hotel. Nita wants to send her friends a drawing of the logo. The owner says that you don't really have to draw all of the logo. Is he right? Is there a way to draw half of the design or less and give instructions for creating the rest by transformations?

Challenge 3

The Riverside Hotel has mixed up the learners' luggage. Help them find the owner of each bag.

Clues

- Nita does not have the smallest bag.
- Mateo's bag is between Nita's and Li's.
- Li does not like yellow or grey.
- Kim does not like yellow or orange.
- Thandi does not have a blue bag.
- Mateo does not have a pink bag.
- Nita's bag is between Thandi's and Kim's.

Challenge 4

The Riverside Hotel has a few rugs that each measure 50 cm by 80 cm. The owner wants to arrange them to make a larger carpet.

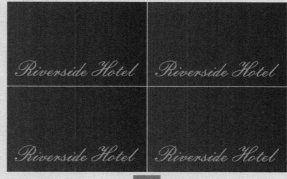

Riverside Hotel *Riverside Hotel*

Riverside Hotel *Riverside Hotel*

Add more this way

Add more this way

a The owner places rugs in a 2 by 2 arrangement. How long are the sides of this carpet?

b What is the area of the carpet with the 2 by 2 arrangement?

c How many more rugs does he need to add to make a 3 by 3 carpet?

d How long are the sides of a 3 by 3 carpet?

e What is the area of a 3 by 3 carpet?

f How many more rugs does he need to add to make a 4 × 4 carpet?

g How long are the sides of a 4 by 4 carpet?

h What is the area of a 4 by 4 carpet?

i Look at your answers. What patterns do you see as these carpets get bigger?

j Can a square carpet ever be made like this?

Challenge 5

Mateo watches a movie at the hotel. In the film, the spy heroine has been captured. Her assistant helps her to escape. The assistant bakes nine identical-looking cakes and hides the key to the prison in one of them. The heroine makes a two-pan balance, and finds the cake with the key by weighing the cakes.

a How will the heroine find the cake that contains the key by weighing the cakes?

b How did the heroine find the right cake in only two lots of weighing?

c If it takes the heroine an average of 40 seconds to weigh two cakes, what is the shortest time she could take to find the key?

Challenge 6

The owner of *The 17th Horse Café* told the learners the story behind its odd name.

'Once, a wise man was riding his horse when he saw a confused farmer. "I have sold my 17 horses," the farmer said. "One customer has bought $\frac{1}{2}$ of the herd, a second customer has bought $\frac{1}{3}$ and a third customer has bought $\frac{1}{9}$. But now I can't see how to divide the herd that way!" The wise man said "add my horse to the herd while you divide". When the farmer did this, he could divide the herd. The wise man's horse was left over, so he rode away.'

Kim is trying to understand how that is possible. Can you explain it to her?

Challenge 7

The 17th Horse Café will give a free dinner to anyone who can start at one of the two hotels, cross every bridge just once, and end at the café. Nobody has been able to do it. Try yourself to see why.

a Mateo thinks he could start from Riverside Hotel and win the free dinner, if only there were an eighth bridge. Where should the eighth bridge go for Mateo's plan to work?

b Caleb likes Mateo's plan. But he says he would build a ninth bridge, and then it would only be possible to win by starting from the Bridges Hotel. Where should this ninth bridge go?

c It takes two minutes plus the number of the bridge doubled to cross each bridge. How much time does it take to cross all nine bridges? Estimate your answer first before calculating it. How close was your estimate?

Challenge 8

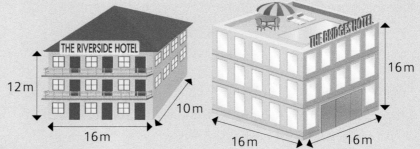

Compare The Riverside Hotel and The Bridges Hotel.

a Which hotel has the larger perimeter? Which has the larger floor area?

b A warehouse exactly the same size as The Bridges Hotel is to be painted. Only the four walls of the warehouse and its entrance doorway are to be painted, and it has no windows. Estimate how many pots of paint will be needed? (A pot of paint can cover 100 square metres of wall with one coat. Each wall needs two coats.)

c How many fewer pots of paint would it take to paint a warehouse the same size as the Riverside Hotel?

d The Bridges Hotel is a cube. What 3-D shape is The Riverside Hotel, approximately?

e Each hotel has a floodlight every 4 m along the wall. How many more floodlights does the hotel with the larger perimeter need?

6a Place value

Explore

What do you notice about this calculator? Which number is missing?
Which possible calculations give the answer shown?

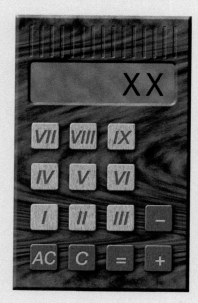

Roman numerals originated in ancient Rome and were used to represent numbers.

Numbers are formed by combining seven different symbols.

I	V	X	L	C	D	M
1	5	10	50	100	500	1 000

How do you think the numbers will be written for 10 to 20?

Many symbols had to be used for larger numbers.
2 789 is shown as MMDCCLXXXIX.

We use the Hindu–Arabic system. It was invented between the first and fourth century by Indian mathematicians and is the most common system for representing numbers in the world. Can you think why?

Place value

Hundred thousands	Ten thousands	Thousands	Hundreds	Tens	Units	Tenths	Hundredths
•• ••	••• ••		•• ••	•• •	•• ••		
	•• ••	•• ••		•• ••	••• ••	•• ••	
				• •	•• •• •	• •	•• ••

Write and then read each of the numbers represented on the place value grid.
The digit 4 appears in each of the numbers. What is its value each time?

One of the numbers can be partitioned into 40 000 + 5 000 + 40 + 3 + 0.4.
Which number is it? Try partitioning the other numbers in the same way.

450 434 is greater than 45 043.4. This can be shown as 450 434 > 45 043.4
Show which is less: 24.24 or 24.25.

1 Partition the numbers to show the value of each digit.

  a 2 092   b 20 920   c 20 920.5

  d 520 905.2   e 502 509.25   f 50.02

2 Replace the ⭐ with one of the symbols >, < or = to make the following statements true.

  a 1 000 ⭐ 10 000   b 1 000 000 ⭐ 100 000   c 10 002.01 ⭐ 100 002.01

  d 27.0 ⭐ 27.00   e 1 000 ⭐ 999.99   f 10 002.10 ⭐ 10 002.01

How can you arrange all four digits in each bag to make:
- the two largest possible numbers?
- an even number in one bag and a multiple of five in the other?
- the two smallest possible odd numbers?
- two numbers that could be used in this statement:
  8 400 < ☐ < ☐ < 9 400

What other numbers can you make?

Multiplying and dividing by 10, 100 and 1000

Learn

Compare the heights of the two animals.
How many times taller is this elephant than the meerkat?

3.1 m

0.31 m

[Not to scale]

A tree measures 31 m in height.
It is 10 times taller than the elephant because 3.1 × 10 = 31.
It is 100 times taller than the meerkat because 0.31 × 100 = 31.
The meerkat is 100 times shorter than the tree because 31 ÷ 100 = 0.31.

You can compare the heights on a place value grid.

Hundreds	Tens	Units	Tenths	Hundredths
		0	3	1
		3	1	
	3	1	0	

Look at the position of the digits each time as the number 0.31 becomes 10 times or 100 times larger.

Now compare these heights with a tower measuring 310 m.

Practise

1 Use what you know about place value to complete these calculations.

Check your answers using a place value grid.

a 2 022 × 10

b 2 022 ÷ 100

c 520 × 100

d 5 200 ÷ 10 × 100

e 25 × 1 000

f 25 × 100 × 10

2 Multiply these numbers mentally. Give each answer to 2 decimal places. The first one has been done for you.

a 9.60 × 10 = 96.00

b 9.60 × 100 =

c 7.07 × 100 =

d 123.09 × 10 =

e 123.00 × 100 =

f 581.02 × 100 =

g $528.91 × 10 =

h $0.99 × 100 =

i $7 136.11 × 100 =

j $9 270.31 × 100 =

3 Use the clues to find out the distance from Nita's home town to three different locations.

Location A	Location B	Location C	Location D
		0.45 km	

- The distance to location B is 1 000 times further than the distance to location C.
- The distance to location D is 10 times closer than to location A.
- Nita and her family go to location A to visit friends and then drive home. The total distance they travel is 90 km.

Try this

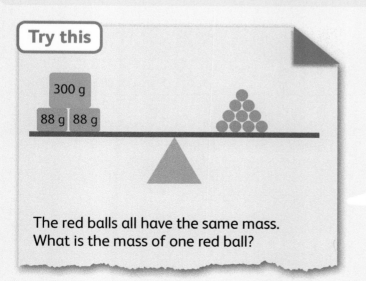

The red balls all have the same mass.
What is the mass of one red ball?

Ordering and comparing positive and negative numbers

Learn

You can use a number line to compare positive and negative numbers. Remember that negative numbers get smaller as they move further away from zero.

Temperatures lower than 0°C are given a negative value. For example: −3°C is colder than 3°C.

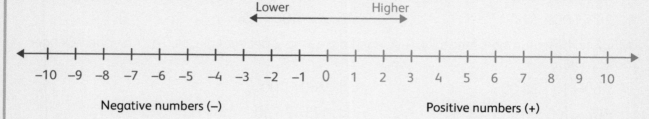

You can compare positive and negative numbers using the greater than (>) and less than (<) symbols. For example, −5 < −3 because −5 is further away from zero than −3.

How do you know that these statements are true?   −2 > −4   −2 < 4

Practise

1 What are the numbers marked at A, B, C, D and E?

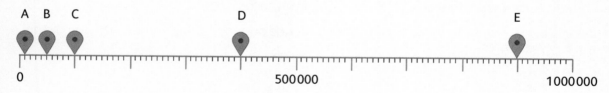

2 What are the numbers marked at A, B, C, D, E and F?

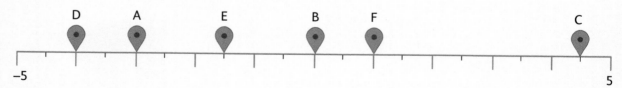

3 a Choose a pair of numbers from question 1 to complete this statement.

 > ☐

b Choose a pair of numbers from question 2 to complete this statement.

 < ☐

6b Rounding and estimating

Key words
approximately

Explore

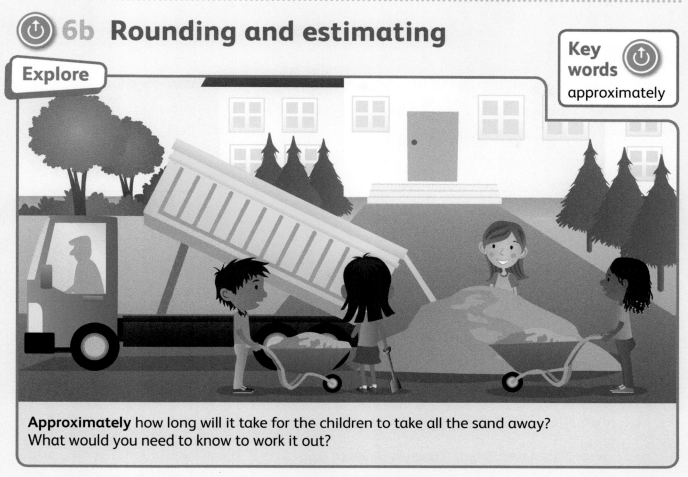

Approximately how long will it take for the children to take all the sand away?
What would you need to know to work it out?

Rounding whole numbers and decimals

Learn

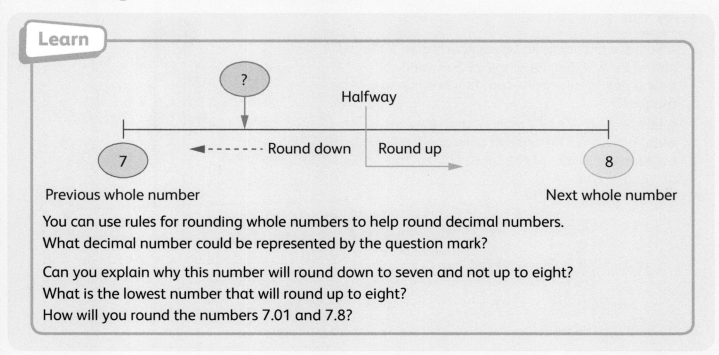

You can use rules for rounding whole numbers to help round decimal numbers.
What decimal number could be represented by the question mark?

Can you explain why this number will round down to seven and not up to eight?
What is the lowest number that will round up to eight?
How will you round the numbers 7.01 and 7.8?

Practise

1 Round these numbers and quantities as shown. The first one has been done for you.

   a 2 547 to the nearest 10 2 550 (because 2 547 is larger than 2 545, so it rounds up to the next 10)

   b 2 54.7 to the nearest whole number

   c 2 547 to the nearest 100

   d 25.47 to the nearest whole number

   e 25.74 to the nearest whole number

2 The following capacities are shown on the measuring jug:

| 1.48 ℓ | 0.75 ℓ | 1.99 ℓ | 0.41 ℓ | 1.12 ℓ |

   a Match each capacity to the correct letter on the jug.

   b Round each capacity to the nearest tenth of a litre.
     For example, a capacity of 3.48 ℓ will round up to 3.5 ℓ.

3 a Order these masses from lightest to heaviest.

| 46.07 kg | 47.6 kg | 74.6 kg | 46.75 kg | 40.7 kg |

   b Now round each mass to the nearest kilogram (kg).

Try this

A school wants to build tennis courts on a plot of land 56.5 m long and 26.5 m wide. How many tennis courts can they build on this plot?

A tennis court is 23.77 m long and 10.97 m wide. There must be a gap of at least 4.5 m between the insides of the courts side to side and end to end.

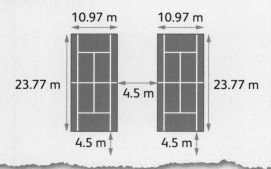

Think like a mathematician

When you are deciding how to estimate and round measurements, think about the units. You might not mind walking or driving an extra 100 m, but an extra 100 km would be different!

6c # Addition and subtraction, including decimal numbers

Explore

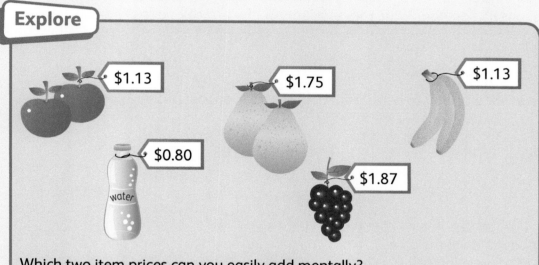

Key words

whole number
approximate
difference
negative

Which two item prices can you easily add mentally?

Which three item prices can you easily add mentally?

How about four item prices?

Can you think of a possible price for oranges that you could also easily add mentally with the other items listed here?

Adding and subtracting decimal numbers

Learn

Look at these calculations. What do you notice about them?

6.3 + 3.7 = 10	10 − 3.7 = 6.3
0.63 + 0.37 = 1	1 − 0.37 = 0.63
63 + 37 = 100	100 − 37 = 63
630 + 370 = 1000	1 000 − 370 = 630

Look at these calculations. What do you notice about them?

7.8 + 2.3 = ?	? − 3.8 = 6.3
0.78 + 0.23 = ?	? − 0.38 = 0.63
78 + 23 = ?	? − 38 = 63
780 + 230 = ?	? − 380 = 630

75

Practise

1 Are these calculations true or false? Write the correct answer for any calculations that are false.

a 6. 8 + 3.2 = 10	c 3.4 + 6.6 = 10	e 9.1 + 1.9 = 10	g 6.6 + 4.4 = 10
b 6.7 + 3.3 = 10	d 0.35 + 0.65 = 1	f 0.91 + 0.09 = 1	h 0.42 + 0.68 = 1

2 Use place value and number facts to help you to do these calculations.

a 560 + 440 =

b 560 + 270 =

c 5.60 + 3.50 =

d 5.60 − 3.50 =

e 0.87 + 0.13 =

f 1.02 − 0.15 =

g 1.87 + 0.37 =

h 2.1 − 1.8 =

3 You can add decimal numbers in any order you like, just as you can for whole numbers. Do these calculations. Change the order in which you add the numbers to make it easier. The first one has been done for you.

a 12 + 17 + 8 = Reorder as 12 + 8 + 17 to give 20 + 17 = 37.

b 1.2 + 1.7 + 0.8 =

c 0.20 + 0.35 + 0.80 =

d $9.99 + $2.50 + $3.50 + $0.01 =

e $4.99 + $3.00 + $3.00 + $3.00 + $3.00 + $3.00 =

Try this

$ 0.99	$ 0.23	$ 0.60	$ 1.25
$ 2.75	$ 1.01	$ 1.25	$ 1.63
$ 1.25	$ 0.37	$ 1.40	$ 0.99

Add three or four numbers together each time.

Find at least five different totals to make this statement true.

$3.70 < ☐ < $4.50

Think like a mathematician

Adding the same number many times is the same as multiplying. For example:

5 + 5 + 5 + 5 is the same as 5 × 4.

So, if you add a list of numbers and keep seeing the same amount, turn part of the calculation into a multiplication. For example:

$3.00 + $5.50 + $3.00 + $7.50 + $3.00 + $3.00

is the same as:

4 × $3.00 + $7.50 + $5.50 =
            $12.00 + $13.00 = $25.00

Using rounding for calculating and estimating

Learn

Mateo uses a rounding and adjusting method to calculate 3 127 + 2 998.
He draws a number line to help him.

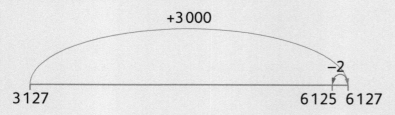

What is the answer to the calculation?
How do you know?

How will Mateo show 3 127 − 2 998 on a number line
using this method?

Will he still need to subtract 2 to reach his answer?

What calculation should he use to check his answer?

I have added 3 000 but I only needed to add 2 998 so I then subtract 2. Am I correct?

$31.27 + $29.98

What would be a good estimate for Nita's calculation?
Why?

Here is the number line that Nita used to help her.

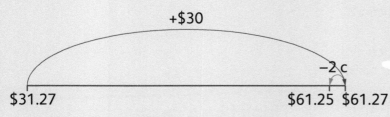

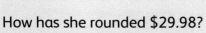

I am also using a rounding and adjusting method to help me add an amount of money

How has she rounded $29.98?

Why did she need to subtract two cents?

Practise

1 Complete these calculations using the rounding and adjusting method.

Remember to check your answers using the inverse.

  a 3 127 + 2 997   b 4 127 − 3 997   c 3 127 + 3 002   d 4 127 − 4 002

  e $14.50 + $ 3.95   f $14.50 − $3.95   g $24.50 + $14.05   h $14.50 − $4.05

2 Complete these calculations.

Remember to make an estimate each time. Will the actual answer be greater or less than your estimate?

  a 56 + 9

  $56.00 + $9.00

  $56.99 + $9.01

  $56.99 + $131.01

  b 176 − 63

  276 − 163

  $12.76 − $1.63

  $12.75 − $1.62

  c 5 678 − 1 996

  5 678 + 1 996

  1 678 + 5 996

  $16.78 + $49.96

3 Mateo's uncle wants to buy three books that cost $9.99, $8.99 and $6.69.

  a Will $25 be enough to pay for the books?

  b He sees another book for $5.49. Will $30 be enough to pay for all four books?

4 a Estimate the total bill.

  b Calculate the total bill using a method of your choice.

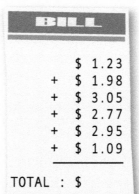

```
         BILL

            $  1.23
      +     $  1.98
      +     $  3.05
      +     $  2.77
      +     $  2.95
      +     $  1.09
          _____

  TOTAL  : $
```

Try this

Place the numbers in the diagram so that:

- each set of three numbers joined by a horizontal line total a number that rounds to 2 600 to the nearest 100
- all pairs of numbers joined by a vertical line have a difference that rounds to 100 to the nearest 100.

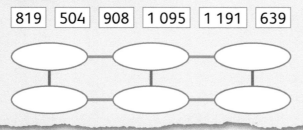

Think like a mathematician

Remember that when you use the rounding and adjusting strategy, you need to ask yourself whether you have added or subtracted too much or not enough.

Differences with negative numbers

Learn

The difference between 4 and 2 is 2. It is the same as asking 'what is 4 – 2?'.

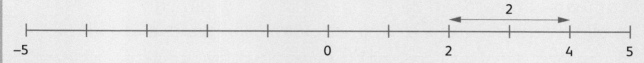

The difference between 4 and –2 is more than 2, because one number is positive and the other negative. So you have to go beyond zero to get from one to the other. It is useful to stop at zero to help you find the difference

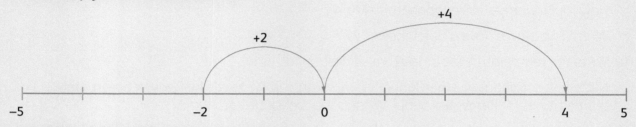

The difference between 4 and –2 is 6.

The difference between the temperatures 4°C and –2°C is 6° so –2°C is 6° colder than 4°C.

I think that the difference between the temperatures –4°C and 2°C will also be 6°? What do you think?

Practise

1 Calculate the differences between these numbers. Use the number line to help you.

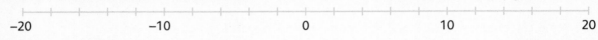

$$-20 \qquad -10 \qquad 0 \qquad 10 \qquad 20$$

  a   10 and 0   b   10 and −2   c   12 and −2   d   −20 and 0

  e   −20 and 2   f   −20 and −2   g   −12 and 8   h   12 and −8

2 Nita and Mateo are finding out about January temperatures in different places around the world.

Minsk	Rome	Mexico City	Singapore	Oslo	Hanoi	Seoul
−4° C	5° C	21°C	26° C	−7° C	15° C	−9°C

  a   How much warmer is Singapore than Minsk?

  b   Which two places have a difference of 22°?

  c   Write the temperatures in order from coldest to hottest.

  d   Nita finds out about another January temperature. It is exactly halfway between the temperatures for Rome and Seoul. What is the temperature?

3 Put these numbers in order of how far they are away from −2 on a number line. Start with the number closest to −2.

0, −1, 2, −3, −7, 6, 1

Try this

Nita runs in a 3 km cross-country race. The course goes uphill and downhill. There are checkpoints on the course at 0.5 km, 1 km, 2 km and 3 km. Here are the measurements of the course and the height at different points.

Distance run (km)	Height change since last checkpoint (m)
Start	0
0.5	−11
1	+6
2	−34
3 (finish)	+44

  a   How much higher or lower is the end of the course than the start?

  b   At what distance is the lowest point in the course?

  c   At what distance is the highest point in the course?

  d   If the start is 159 m above sea level, how high is the 1 km checkpoint?

Solving problems

Learn

Look at this problem.

Kim cuts different lengths of ribbon for her kites.
She uses two of these ribbons. What is the
shortest total length she could have?

The shortest total length must be made using the
two shortest ribbons.

The bar model represents the problem. What does
the question mark represent?

0.65 m	1.35 m
?	

1.98 m   0.65 m   1.35 m   1.5 m

Which strategy will you use to calculate 0.65 m + 1.35 m? Can you use any number bonds to help you?

The shortest total length using two ribbons is 2 m or 200 cm.

What is the longest total length using two ribbons? How will you represent the problem using
bars this time?

Practise

1 Use the ribbon lengths from the *Learn* activity to solve these problems.

 a Kim uses three ribbons. What different total lengths could she have? Find two possible answers.

 b What is the total length of all four ribbons?

 c How much longer is the total length of all four ribbons than the length of the shortest ribbon?

2 Is there a mistake in this bill? If it is wrong, what is the correct total?

3 Which numbers could replace the ★ and ◆ symbols to make this
calculation correct?

 ★ + 475 = 1 ◆ 24

 Find at least three different answers.

4 Mateo has a toy car that he winds up by pulling it backwards and
then letting it go. Mateo puts the car at the zero mark on a tape
measure, pulls it back 5 cm and lets it go. It stops at the 67 cm
mark on the tape measure. How far did it travel?

BILL	
	$1.99
	$7.23
	$4.77
	$3.99
TOTAL	$19.78

Self-check

A Place value

1 Do these multiplications:
   a $1.23 \times 10 =$
   b $1.23 \times 100 =$
   c $1.23 \times 1000 =$
   d $1.23 \div 10 =$

2 Answer the questions about this group of numbers:
   0, −12, −5, 24, 1 000
   a If the numbers were placed on a number line, which number would be furthest left? Which number would be furthest right?
   b Write the numbers out in order, using the < or > signs to show the relationships between them. Start from the smallest number, going to the largest number.

3 Answer these questions about our number system.
   a What is our number system called?
   b Name three good things about our number system.

B Rounding and estimating

1 Round these numbers as instructed.
   a 362 to the nearest hundred
   b 362 to the nearest ten
   c 3.62 to the nearest whole number
   d 3.62 to the nearest tenth

2 Put each of these sets of quantities in order, from smallest to largest.
   a 1.73 ℓ, 1.37 ℓ, 1 735 ml
   b 1 234 m, 2.305 km, 12.34 m

C Addition and subtraction, including decimal numbers

1 Do these calculations.
   a $0.23 + 1.77 =$
   b $12 + 0.7 + 8.0 + 0.3 =$
   c $23 + 799 =$
   d $\$4.99 + \$10.00 + \$3.01 =$

2 Find the difference between these temperatures.
   a −10°C and 15°C
   b −15°C and 17°C
   c −9 °C and 9°C
   d −19°C and 9°C

Unit 7   Measures and problem solving

7a The metric system

Explore

Caleb and Thandi have made vinegar rockets.

They mixed vinegar and baking soda in an old plastic cola bottle, and then they put in a cork.

The mixture fizzed, popped the cork, and the bottle shot off up the slide like a rocket.

Key words

distance
metric system
imperial system

They wrote down their results of the distance travelled by each rocket in a table.

Amount of vinegar (in 0.5 ℓ plastic bottle)	Amount of baking soda	How far did the rocket go?
0.100 ℓ	15 g	0 cm (didn't launch)
0.200 ℓ	15 g	580 cm
0.300 ℓ	15 g	100 cm
0.400 ℓ	15 g	20 cm
?	?	?

Predict the results that would go into the blank row.

Make predictions for the distance travelled if these amounts of vinegar are used: 50 ml, 150 ml, 250 ml and 350 ml.

How accurate do you think Thandi and Caleb's measurements were?

Which metric units did they use in their experiment?

What was the best recipe for rocket fuel?

Reading and using decimal units

Learn

A litre is one thousand times bigger than a millilitre. So to convert from litres to millilitres you need to multiply by 1 000 (an easy multiplication using place value).

We can use decimals to write these measurements as litres.

900 ml = 0.900 ℓ = 0.9 ℓ
150 ml = 0.150 ℓ = 0.15 ℓ
195 ml = 0.195 ℓ

Litres — 1.0

—0.5 ℓ

—200 ml

900 ml   150 ml   195 ml

As there are 1 000 ml in 1 ℓ, we need up to 3 decimal places.

Remember that 1.7 km can also be written as 1.70 km or 1.700 km.

Write these measurements using decimals. An example has been done for you.

| | mm and | | m

Weight of carrots in g: 500 g
Convert into kg:

$$\frac{500 \text{ g}}{1\,000\text{g}} = 0.5 \text{ kg}$$

| | g and | | kg

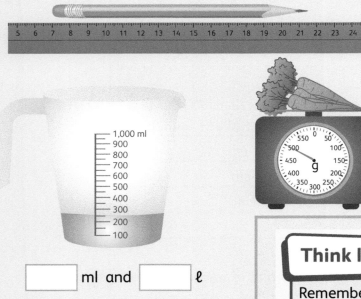

| | ml and | | ℓ

Think like a mathematician

Remember, there are clues in the words for units. They can tell you what the conversions are:
- 'Milli-' means one thousandth of a bigger unit.
- 'Centi-' means one hundredth of a bigger unit.
- 'Kilo-' means a thousand times a smaller unit.

Practise

1   Write the height of each mountain in km.

Mountain	Height in metres (m)
Mauna Kea	4 205 m
Mont Blanc	4 809 m
Everest	8 848 m
Aconagua	6 962 m
Mount Fuji	3 776 m
Ben Nevis	1 345 m

Mount Everest is 8 848 m high

2   Kim weighs her bags before going on an aeroplane.

   a   Write all the weights in both grams and kilograms.

   b   Her allowance is 5.5 kg. Has she packed too much?

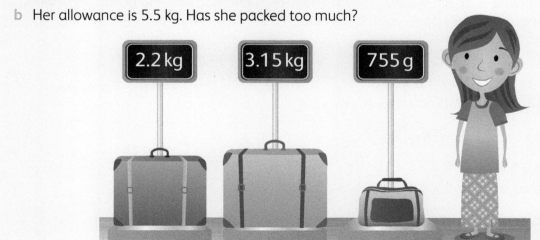

2.2 kg   3.15 kg   755 g

3

Soup recipe

Serves 4 people.

250 g of potatoes

130 g of carrots

50 g of onion

700 ml of stock

130 ml of cream

Here is my delicious soup recipe.

a   Mateo needs to make enough soup for 6 people. Write the recipe using kg and ℓ for the measurements.

b   Write the soup recipe to serve 10 people.

Try this

Measure the length and width of your classroom and your playground. Then write the measurements in km.

Metric and imperial measures of length

Learn

The **imperial system** is an old system of measure that is still used in some parts of the world. It measures length in inches, feet, yards and miles.

1 mile = 1.6 km and 1 km = 0.62 miles

How many km is 5 miles? $5 \times 1.6 = 8$ km
How many miles is 15 km? $15 \times 0.62 = 9.3$ miles

1 inch = 2.5 cm and 1 cm = 0.4 inches

How many cm is 6 inches? $6 \times 2.5 = 15$ cm
How many inches is 5 cm? $5 \times 0.4 = 2$ inches

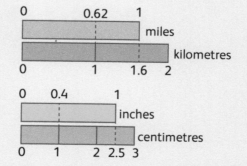

Other imperial units: 12 inches make 1 foot, 3 feet make 1 yard, 1 760 yards make 1 mile.

Metric and imperial measures of length

1 Measure some classroom items in cm.
Now create a table to show the length of each item
in cm and inches. Use this table as a guideline.

Object	Length in cm	Length in inches
Pencil	10 cm	
Ruler	30 cm	12 inches

2 Are these statements true or false? If a
statement is false, write down the correct version.

a An inch is more than a centimetre

b A kilometre is less than a mile

c 1 inch = 2.5 cm

d 1 mile = 1.6 kg

e 10 cm = 4 inches

f 16 miles = 10 km

g 20 inches = 5 cm

h 16 km = 10 miles

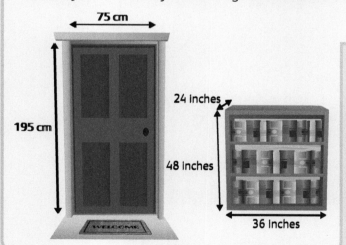

3 Nita's grandfather has given her a bookcase. Will the bookcase fit through the doorway?
Prove your answer by converting all the measures as accurately as you can.

75 cm

195 cm

24 inches

48 inches

36 inches

Try this

Draw a plan of your classroom, and give
the measurements in yards, feet and inches.

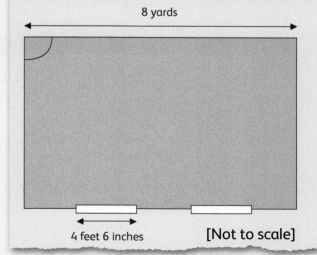

8 yards

4 feet 6 inches

[Not to scale]

Think like a mathematician

Remember, when you are problem solving, you
must make sure that all of the measurements
are in the same units before you can add,
subtract, multiply, or divide.

7b **Length, area and perimeter**

Explore

Use the scale to find a measure for the area of this garden.

Key words

opposite

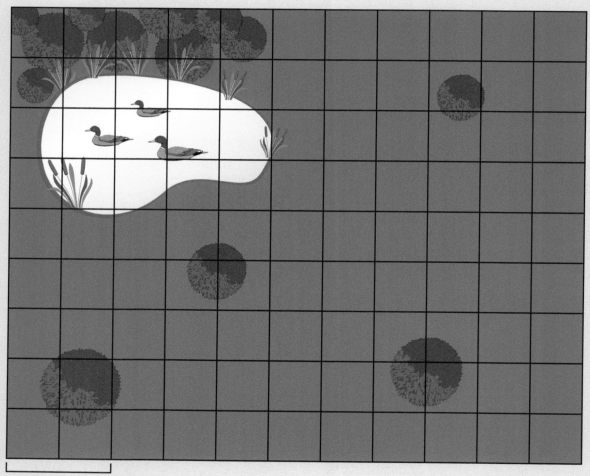

1 m

> How big is this garden without the pond?

Nita wants to work out the area of this garden without counting the pond.

What is the best estimate you can make?

Different methods for compound shapes

Learn

You can work out the missing lengths by using a subtraction.

The opposite sides of a rectangle must be the same length so ? + 3 = 5, which means ? = 2

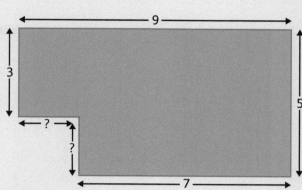

The compound shape can be split into two rectangles.

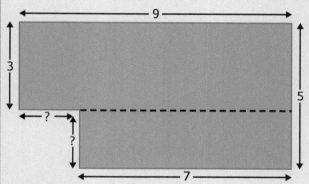

9 − 7 = 2

Area of compound rectangle

7 × 5 = 35

2 × 3 = 6

Total area = 35 + 6 = 41

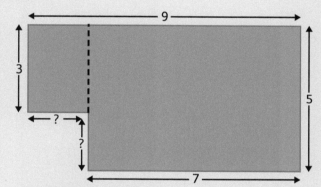

Missing length = 5 − 3 = 2

Area of shape:

7 × 2 = 14

9 × 3 = 27

Total area = 14 + 27 = 41

Or you can think of it as one large rectangle with a smaller shape cut away.

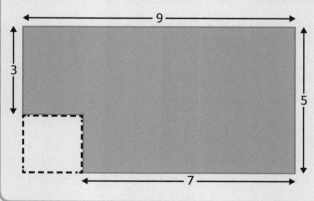

Area of large rectangle: 9 × 5 = 45

Area of part removed: 2 × 2 = 4

Total area = 45 − 4 = 41

[The drawings on this page are not drawn to scale.]

Practise

1 Find the perimeter of each shape. Use two different methods to find the areas.

a

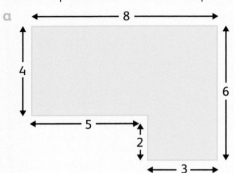

b

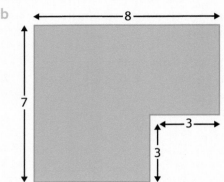

2 Mateo and Nita have four rectangles like this. They cut each one into two shapes.

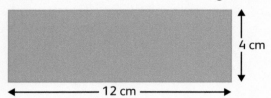

Calculate the area of each new shape. Work out the perimeter of the two new shapes that have been cut out.

a

b

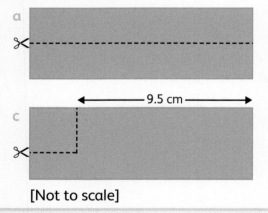

c

d

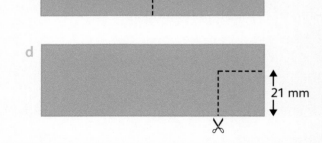

[Not to scale]

Try this

Make a rectangle with the same dimensions as the one in Practise question 2. Cut it into two shapes.

Find a solution so that the area of one of the new shapes has double the area of the other.

Find another solution so that one of the areas is triple the area of the other shape.

Find out how to cut your rectangle so that one of the new shapes has half the perimeter of the other new shapes.

7c Time

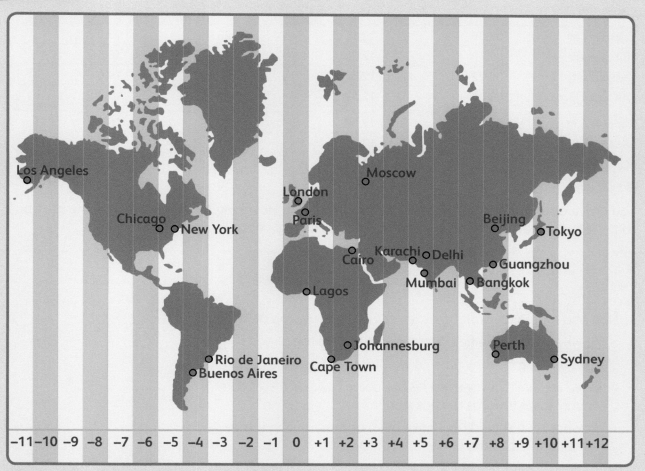

| −11 | −10 | −9 | −8 | −7 | −6 | −5 | −4 | −3 | −2 | −1 | 0 | +1 | +2 | +3 | +4 | +5 | +6 | +7 | +8 | +9 | +10 | +11 | +12 |

What is the time now where you live?

Where in the world is it night-time?

How long until it will be midday in the cities marked on the map?

What is the time now in Sydney?

What time will it be in Chicago, when it is 1 p.m. in Mumbai?

Make up three questions to ask your class about time differences. For example "What is the time in Cape Town when it is …"

Key words

timetable

time zone

weeks

months

duration

Timetables

> ## Learn
>
> | | | | | |
> |---|---|---|---|---|
> | Bus station | 08:56 | 12:11 | 15:26 | 18:41 |
> | City centre | 09:10 | 12:25 | 15:40 | 18:55 |
> | Railway station | 09:22 | 12:37 | 15:52 | 19:07 |
> | Airport | 09:37 | 12:52 | 16:07 | 19:22 |
>
> | | | | | |
> |---|---|---|---|---|
> | Airport | 09:43 | 12:58 | 16:13 | 19:28 |
> | Railway station | 09:53 | 13:08 | 16:23 | 19:38 |
> | City centre | 10:03 | 13:18 | 16:33 | 19:48 |
> | Bus station | 10:20 | 13:35 | 16:50 | 20:05 |
>
> You arrive at the airport at 4 o'clock in the afternoon. How long must you wait for the next bus to the city centre? At what time will you get to the city centre?

> ## Practise
>
> 1 Nita and Mateo are waiting at the city centre bus stop at 10.00.
>
>   a At what time is the first bus they can take to the airport?
>
>   b For how long do they have to wait for the bus to the airport?
>
>   c Which bus will they see first? A bus going towards the airport, or one going towards the bus station?
>
>   d At what time should they have been at the bus stop if they wanted to get to the airport by 10:00?
>
> 2. Some new buses have been added to the bus route. They travel at the same speed as the other buses. Copy and complete the timetable.
>
>
>
> | | | | | |
> |---|---|---|---|---|
> | Bus station | 10.29 | | | |
> | City centre | | | 17.44 | |
> | Railway station | | | | 23.59 |
> | Airport | | 14.57 | | |
>
> 3 It is Mateo's birthday. His aunt and his cousins want to treat him to lunch in the city centre. His aunt can arrive at the airport at 11:45. One cousin can arrive by train at 11:00, 12:00 or 13:00. Another cousin can be at the bus station at 9:30 or 11:30. Using the bus timetable, work out at what time they can have lunch together.

Try this

It is not the same time in every part of the world. When it is noon in London, it is 3 p.m. in Abu Dhabi and 7 a.m. in New York. Some timetables, like those for airlines or international trains, have to take this into account. We use **time zones** to know what the time is in different parts of the world. Look at the time zones on the world map on page 91.

a What time is it in Mumbai when it is noon in London?

b It takes 5 and a half hours to fly from Johannesburg to Rio. The flight leaves at 18.30 in Johannesburg. What is the time in Rio when it lands?

c If it is 9.00 a.m. in Sydney, write the times in: Los Angeles, Chicago, Buenos Aires, Cairo and Guangzhou.

Calendars

Learn

February						
Sun	Mon	Tue	Wed	Thu	Fri	Sat
			1	2	3	4
5	6	7	8	9	10	11
12	13	14	15	16	17	18
19	20	21	22	23	24	25
26	27	28				

March						
Sun	Mon	Tue	Wed	Thu	Fri	Sat
			1	2	3	4
5	6	7	8	9	10	11
12	13	14	15	16	17	18
19	20	21	22	23	24	25
26	27	28	29	30	31	

April						
Sun	Mon	Tue	Wed	Thu	Fri	Sat
						1
2	3	4	5	6	7	8
9	10	11	12	13	14	15
16	17	18	19	20	21	22
23	24	25	26	27	28	29
30						

Calendars give us information about days and dates.

With a calendar you can answer questions like these:

● What day was 15th January?

● What is the date 100 days after 1st February?

Practise

Use the calendar on page 93 to answer these questions.

1 a   Nita's birthday is on 1st May. On which day of the week will it be?

b   Mateo's birthday is on 1st January. Which day of the week was it on? And on which day of the week will it be on in the next year?

2   Gardening club is on Mondays at school.

Type of seed	When to plant	Time until fully grown
Sunflower	February	12 weeks
Lettuce	Late March – Early April	10 – 12 weeks
Carrot	Late February – Early March	12 – 16 weeks

a   Suggest suitable dates on which to plant each set of seeds.

b   Now write dates for when the plants should be fully grown. Show the earliest and latest dates.

3 a   The school has a sports day on the last Friday in May. What is the date of that day?

b   Nita is going to visit her cousin on the first weekend in September. Write the dates of those days.

Think like a mathematician

When you are working out **duration** in days, you should think about whether to include the start date and end date.
For example, imagine today is Monday, 6th March. Mateo is given some homework. It will take him seven evenings to do the homework. He must hand in the work on Monday morning, 13th March. He can't count the evening of 13th March, so he had better start today!

Try this

Work out the day of the week on which your next birthday will fall. Think carefully about the number of days in each month.

Self-check

A The metric system

1 Do these conversions.
   a 1.755 m to cm
   b 334 ml to ℓ
   c 1.27 kg to g

2 How long is this cable in centimetres? How long is it in inches?

B Length, area and perimeter

1 A rectangle is 7 cm long and 5 cm wide. Calculate its area and perimeter.

2 A white square has been placed on top of a pink rectangle.

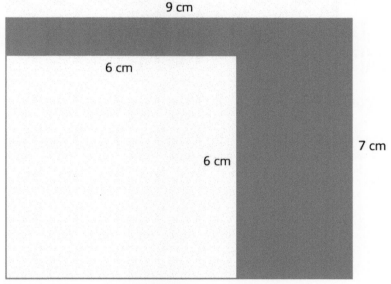

9 cm

6 cm

6 cm

7 cm

   a What are the area and the perimeter of the white square?
   b What are the area and the perimeter of the parts of the pink rectangle that can still be seen?

C Time

1 Use the bus timetable on page 92 to say whether these statements are **true** or **false**.
   a If Mateo is at the airport at 4 o'clock in the afternoon, he will have to wait less than 15 minutes for a bus.
   b A bus leaves the bus station just before a quarter to eight in the evening.
   c If Nita is at the airport at 8 o'clock in the evening, it is too late for her to catch a bus to the city centre.

2 Use the calendar on page 93 to answer these questions:
   a How many weeks are there between 23rd February and 5th April?
   b What date is five days before 1st April?

Unit 8 Number and problem solving

⟳ 8a Factors and multiples

Explore

Nita can ask twenty questions to work out which number Mateo is thinking of.
He can only answer 'yes' or 'no'.
What number could it be? What other questions could Nita ask to find the number?

Factors and multiples

Learn

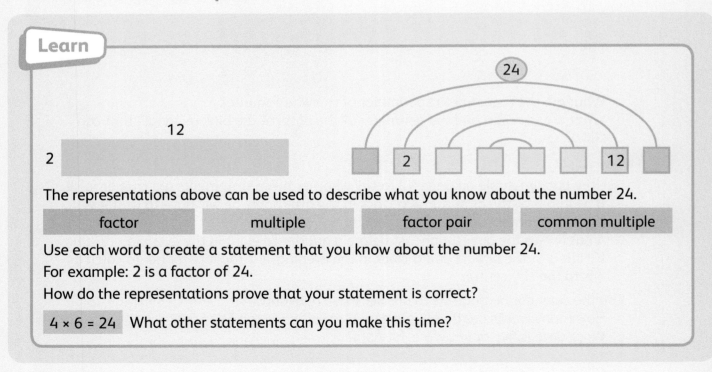

The representations above can be used to describe what you know about the number 24.

| factor | multiple | factor pair | common multiple |

Use each word to create a statement that you know about the number 24.
For example: 2 is a factor of 24.
How do the representations prove that your statement is correct?

$4 \times 6 = 24$ What other statements can you make this time?

Practise

1

Here is a factor pair for 48.

How many other factor pairs can you find to add to the diagram?

2

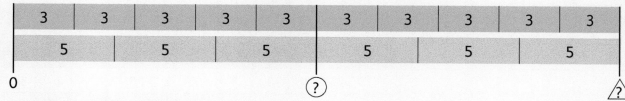

a What is the value of the circle?

b What is the value of the triangle?

c Is this statement true or false? How do you know?

> The values of the circle and the triangle are common multiples of 3 and 5.

d What are the next two common multiples of 3 and 5? What do you notice?

3 Find all the common multiples of 2 and 3 up to 30. Show how you worked them out. Why can you be sure that you have found them all?

Try this

Nita has a total of 325 cents in her money box. All her coins are the same.

Mateo has a total of 250 cents in his money box. All his coins are the same.

Investigate to find out the following:

- Can Nita and Mateo each have the same coins? For example, can they both have only 10 c coins?
- Which coins can Mateo **not** have?
- Which coins can Nita **not** have?
- Which coins can neither have in their money box?

Think like a mathematician

Think about any patterns you know that multiples of 25 or 50 make when you count. How can this help you?

Prime numbers

Learn

The bars represent the numbers 6, 2, 7 and 11 in different ways using their factors.

Which number is the odd one out and why?

6		
3		3
2	2	2
1	1	1	1	1	1

2	
1	1

7						
1	1	1	1	1	1	1

11										
1	1	1	1	1	1	1	1	1	1	1

A prime number has exactly two different factors – itself and one.

So a prime number can only have one factor pair.

Practise

1 Sketch bars to prove which of these numbers are prime.

  a 5

  b 9

  c 13

  d 1

2 Is this statement true or false?

  > 2 is the only even prime number.

  Explain how you know.

3 Prove that 23 is a prime number by systematically checking for its factors.

Try this

I am thinking of a prime number.
It is one less than a common multiple of 4 and 5.
It is one more than a common multiple of 6 and 9.
What number could it be?

8b Number patterns, sequences and generalisations

Explore

Which snake is good at maths? … an adder!!!

Nita tells her favourite maths joke to two friends.
The next day, the friends each tell the joke to two more friends.
On the third day, these friends also tell the joke to two more friends. And so on…

How many children will hear Nita's joke on 7th March?

How many children will have heard the joke in total by this date?

And by 10th March? And by another day in March?

Number sequences

Learn

87   43

The difference between the terms in this sequence is the same prime number.
How can you work out the rule for this sequence?

The digits in each number make another pattern in this sequence.
Can you use the pattern to find the value of the second yellow circle in the sequence?
Check your answer using the rule.

Practise

1 a How can you prove this statement without listing the rest of the terms?

> Zero will not be a term in the sequence in the *Learn* panel on page 99.

   b What is the 10th term in the sequence?

2 Here are some different sequences. Find the rule and the missing terms each time.

   a −20, ___, −12, −8, ___

   b 224, 199, ___, 149, ___

   c ___, 4, ___, 2.4, ___, 0.8

   d $-2\frac{3}{4}$, ___, $-1\frac{3}{4}$, ___, $-\frac{3}{4}$, ___

3 Here are some different sequences.
   Find the rule and sketch the 6th term each time.

   a

   b

   c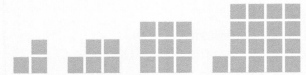

Think like a mathematician

Remember to check to see if the terms increase or decrease by the same amount each time. If they do not, you will need to look for other patterns to help you.

Odd and even numbers

Learn

What do the representations show you about adding pairs of odd and even numbers?

Can you use them to explain what happens when you add an odd and even number?

You can also see that double 3 is 6 and double 4 is 8.

What does that tell you about doubling an odd number and doubling an even number?

This representation shows 3 × 3 or 3 + 3 + 3.

What can you say about multiplying an odd number by an odd number?

Practise

1 Without calculating, decide whether the answers to these calculations will be odd or even. The first one has been done for you.

   a 250 × 10 =

      The answer will be even because even × even = even.

   b 71 × 6 =

   c 1 345 + 45 =

   d 8 764 − 6 422 =

   e 357 839 × 9 =

   f 943 653 − 6 763 =

   g 6 383 303 + 77 =

   h 999 988 − 752 421 =

   i 980 × 7 =

2 Nita thinks of a one-digit number and multiplies it by seven. She adds six to it. Her answer is odd.

  Did Nita start with an odd or an even number? How do you know?

Try this

21 − 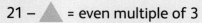 = even multiple of 3

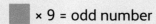 × 9 = odd number

▲ + ■ < 20

The square and the triangle represent two different whole numbers less than 16.

Find a possible value for the square and triangle so that each statement is true.

Now find another possible value for the triangle and the square. And another?

Think like a mathematician

For the *Try this* activity, remember to check that the number you use for the shapes each time works for all of the statements.

8c Multiplication and division

Explore

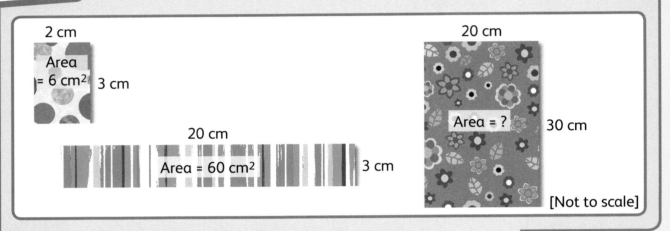

2 cm

Area = 6 cm² 3 cm

20 cm

Area = ? 30 cm

20 cm

Area = 60 cm² 3 cm

[Not to scale]

What is the same and what is different about the size of each of these pieces of cloth? Can you see a pattern that the sizes follow?

What is the area of the largest piece of cloth?

A fourth piece of cloth is cut to fit with this pattern.
What will the dimensions and area of this piece of cloth be?

Key words

partition
recombine
equivalent

Using multiples of 10 and 100 to help multiply

Learn

We can use factors to help us multiply.
How have factors been used in this calculation?

$50 \times 30 = 5 \times 10 \times 3 \times 10$
$= 5 \times 3 \times 100$
$= 15 \times 100$

Using factors in the same way can help when multiplying by a near multiple of ten using the rounding and adjusting method.

$50 \times 29 = 50 \times (30 - 1)$
$= (50 \times 30) - (50 \times 1)$
$= (5 \times 3 \times 10 \times 10) - (50 \times 1)$

29   1   [Not to scale]

50 × 29

50   = 1 500 – 50

= 1 450

Where can you see each part of the calculation in this representation?

50×30 is also a useful estimate for the calculation 50×29.

Practise

1 Are these statements true or false? Correct any statements that are false.

a $80 \times 20 = 8 \times 200$

b $40 \times 40 > 20 \times 80$

c $300 \times 50 = 100 \times 15 \times 10$

d $60 \times 20 \times 20 < 60 \times 40$

e $400 \times 60 = 30 \times 20 \times 40$

f $50 \times 20 < 100 \times 10 < 50 \times 200$

2 What calculations do these arrays represent? What is a useful estimate and the answer for each one?

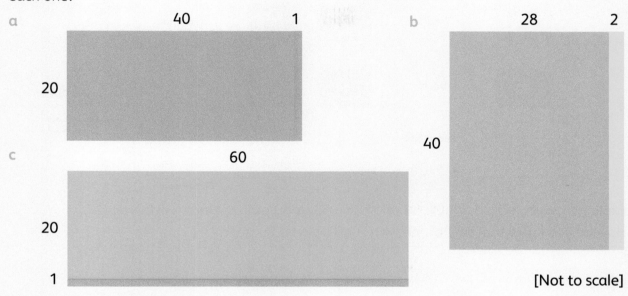

[Not to scale]

3 A truck is loaded with the following:

- 80 bags of cement, each weighing 20 kg
- 40 bags of sand, each weighing 30 kg
- 30 bags of gravel, each weighing 40 kg.

a What is the total weight of the truck's load?

b A second truck loads 81 bags of the cement, 39 bags of the sand and 32 bags of the gravel.

   What is the total weight of the second truck's load?

Think like a mathematician

Remember that finding a factor pair with one factor as 10 or 100 means that you can use your knowledge of place value to help you multiply easily.

Doubling or halving any two-digit number

Learn

You can double or halve any number more easily by partitioning it, then putting it back together:

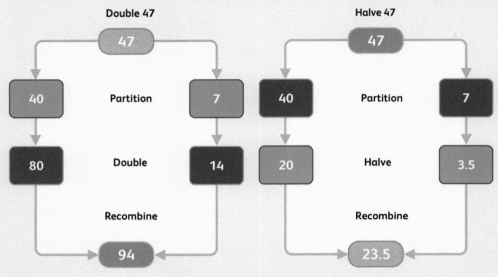

Explain how you would double 59 and halve 59 using partitioning to help you.

How do you know that half of 59 will not be a whole number?

Practise

1 Double and halve each of these numbers.
What patterns do you notice?

| 78 | 39 | 42 | 21 | 3.9 | 0.42 | 84 |

2 Find the value of the triangular shape each time.

a $75 + \triangle + \triangle = 110$

b $74 \times 2 = \triangle$

c $37 + 37 + \triangle = 150$

d $99 \div 2 \div 2 = \triangle$

e $\frac{1}{2}$ of $\triangle = 48$

f double $\triangle = 8.6 \div 2$

3 Here is a soup recipe for 4 people.
Write the recipe for 2 people.

Creamy mushroom soup

1.5 ℓ water
75 g onion
0.24 kg mushrooms
0.15 ml cream
15 g herbs

Try this

Mateo thinks of a number. He doubles it, then adds six.

He halves the answer and then halves it again.

His number is now 8.5.

What number did he start with?

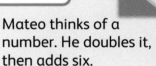

Using factors to help multiply

Learn

You can use what you know about factors of numbers to help make decisions about the easiest way to multiply using a mental method.

$23 \times 6 =$
$23 \times 3 \times 2 =$

$32 \times 8 =$
$32 \times 2 \times 2 \times 2 =$

Why will the two calculations in the pink box give the same answer?
What about the two calculations in the purple box?

These representations help to show how the factors of 6 and 8 have been used to help complete each calculation.

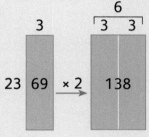

$23 \times 6 = 23 \times 3 \times 2 = 138$

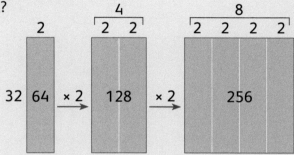

$32 \times 8 = 32 \times 2 \times 2 \times 2 = 256$

Practise

1. Are these statements true or false? Correct any statements that are false.

   a $8 \times 31 = 31 \times 2 \times 2$
   b $7 \times 14 = 7 \times 7 \times 2$
   c $6 \times 15 = 15 \times 3 \times 2$

   d $18 \times 7 = 7 \times 9 \times 2$
   e $14 \times 9 = 8 \times 9 \times 2$
   f $35 \times 20 = 35 \times 2 \times 10$

2. Use factors to help calculate these amounts.
   Remember to make an estimate first. Will your answer be more or less than your estimate?

   a $\$64 \times 4$
   b $\$6 \times 22$
   c $\$12 \times 15$
   d $\$8 \times 54$
   e $\$14 \times 9$

3. Use all the digits 2, 2, 3, 4, 6, 8
   to make this set of statements true.

   $26 \times \boxed{} = 26 \times 2 \times \boxed{}$

   $14 \times \boxed{} = 7 \times \boxed{8} \times \boxed{}$

   $\boxed{} \times 31 = 31 \times \boxed{} \times 2$

Think like a mathematician

Consider which number in each calculation will give you factors that will make the multiplication easier to carry out. For example, 14×6 may be easier as $7 \times 6 \times 2$ than as $14 \times 3 \times 2$.

Making equivalent multiplications

Learn

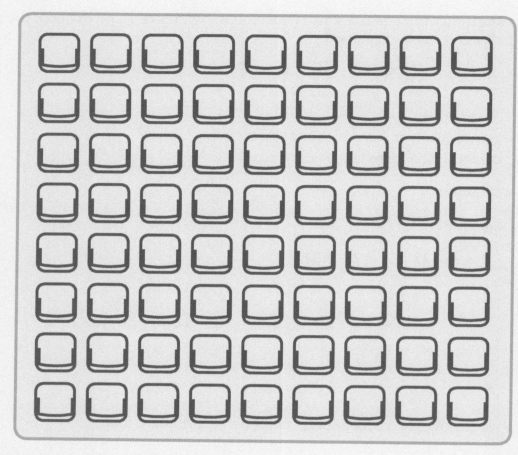

A set of chairs is arranged into 8 rows of 9 chairs.

How can the same number of chairs be arranged in:

a 4 rows?

b 2 rows?

c 1 row?

How many chairs are there each time?

You have made a set of equivalent multiplication calculations by halving one number and doubling the other.

So, $8 \times 9 = 4 \times 18 = 2 \times 36 = 1 \times 72$

The easiest calculation to solve is $1 \times 72 = 72$, as multiplying by 1 has no effect on the number.

Practise

1 Find equivalent calculations to help work out the answers to these multiplications questions.

a 16 × 15   b 8 × 75   c 12 × 15

d 35 × 16   e 62 × 4   f 8 × 12.5

2 Mateo and Nita are investigating capacity. They have the following containers:

- 8 red containers that each hold 2.5 litres of water
- 4 blue containers that each hold double the amount of water of a red container
- 2 green containers that each hold double the amount of water of a blue container
- 1 yellow container that holds double the amount of water of a green container.

a What is the total amount of water that can be held in the same colour containers each time?

b What is the capacity of each blue container?

c What is the capacity of each green container?

d What is the capacity of the yellow container?

e Complete this statement:

The yellow container holds ____ times more water than a red container.

Try this

What is the value of the and the ▲? Check that the values work for all calculations.

■ × ▲ = 120   [■ × 2] × [▲ ÷ 2] = 120

60 × [▲ ÷ 4] = 120   120 × 1 = 120

Using partitioning to help multiply and divide

Learn

I think you can only use partitioning to help with multiplication calculations; not with division.

16 × 22

| | 20 | 2 |

16 | 16 × 20 (15 × 2 × 10) | 16 × 2

$16 \times 22 = (16 \times 20) + (16 \times 2)$
$= 320 + 32$
$= 362$

No, you can use partitioning for division too; but you can only partition the number to be divided.

93 ÷ 7

7

10 | 70 ÷ 7 = 10

} 93

3 | 21 ÷ 7 = 3

r2

$93 \div 7 = 13 \text{ r } 2 \text{ or } 13\frac{2}{7}$
because
$91 \div 7 = (70 \div 7) + (21 \div 7)$
$97 \div 7 = (70 + 21) \div 7$
$\qquad = 10 + 3$
$\qquad = 13$

You can use partitioning to help you break up a calculation into parts that are easier to solve.

Why is 91 partitioned into 70 and 21 in Nita's example rather than 90 and 1?

Practise

1 Use partitoning to complete these calculations.

   Remember to make an estimate first. Will your answer be more or less than your estimate?

   a 23 × 9   b 35 × 7   c 48 × 9   d 52 × 6

   e 63 × 8   f 172 × 7   g 235 × 6   h 4 235 × 6

2 Do these divisions using partitioning. Which calculations do you think will definitely leave a remainder? Why? The first one has been done for you.

   a 51 ÷ 3   51 can be partitioned into 30 and 21. These are both multiples of three so there will be no remainder.
                      51 ÷ 3 = 17

   b 53 ÷ 3

   c 53 ÷ 7   d 87 ÷ 5

   e 79 ÷ 4   f 84 ÷ 9

   g 123 ÷ 10   h 99 ÷ 8

3 How many full weeks and days left over are there each time?

   a 96 days   b 77 days   c 62 days   d 54 days

4 Find the missing masses in the table. Give your answers as mixed numbers.

1 box	a	645 g	c	575 g	e
7 of these boxes	85 kg	b	99 kg	d	64 kg

Try this

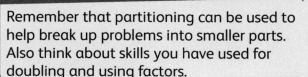

I can use what I know about the multiplication tables for 7 and 10 to help me find the multiplication table for 17.

What do you think Mateo can do?
What facts can he find?

Think like a mathematician

Remember that partitioning can be used to help break up problems into smaller parts. Also think about skills you have used for doubling and using factors.

Dividing larger numbers

Learn

Which of these calculations will leave a remainder? How do you know?

| $775 \div 4$ | $775 \div 25$ | $\$7.75 \div 4$ |

All multiples of 4 are even. A whole number can be divided exactly by 4 when the last two digits are a multiple of 4.

All multiples of 25 end in 25, 50, 75 or are a multiple of 100. So, all whole numbers ending in this way will be exactly divisible by 25.

Look at the written methods that can be used to solve each calculation.

$$\begin{array}{r} 1\ 9\ 3\ \text{r3} \\ 4\overline{\smash{)}7\ ^37\ ^15} \end{array} \qquad \begin{array}{r} 3\ 1 \\ 25\overline{\smash{)}7\ ^77\ ^25} \end{array} \qquad \begin{array}{r} 1.\ 9\ 3\ \text{r3 cents} \\ 4\overline{\smash{)}7.\ ^37\ ^15} \end{array}$$

For the calculation $775 \div 4 = 193 \text{ r } 3$, the remainder may need to be rounded or turned into a fraction depending on the question e.g. $775 \text{ kg} \div 4 = 193\frac{3}{4}$ kg or 193.75 kg

You can check $775 \div 25 = 31$. You know that there are four groups of 25 in 100, so there must be 28 groups (4×7) of 25 in 700, and then three more groups in 75, which is 31 groups in total.

Practise

1   Complete these calculations. First think about any tests of divisibility that you can use to decide which will give a remainder. Check each of your answers using multiplication

    a $444 \div 4 =$ b $925 \div 25 =$ c $297 \div 3 =$ d $348 \div 4 =$ e $301 \div 10 =$

    f $877 \div 5 =$ g $922 \div 3 =$ h $288 \div 12$ i $504 \div 100 =$ j $845 \div 5 =$

2   Answer these money questions.

    a $\$144 \div 12$ b $\$1.56 \div 12$ c   Is $\$75.48$ exactly divisible by four?

    d   How many cents remain when $\$817.87$ is divided by four?

    e   Is $\$235.35$ exactly divisible by 25? If not, how many cents will be left over?

3   a   How many years are there for each number of months shown here?

      i   168 months   ii   384 months   iii   312 months   iv   516 months

    b   How many days are there for each number of hours shown here?

      i   192 hours   ii   264 hours   iii   552 hours   iv   672 hours

4   The bill for a restaurant meal comes to $\$264$.
    Divide the bill between the twelve people at the meal.

Self-check

A Factors and multiples

1 Name three factors of 100.

2 Which of these numbers is not prime? 2, 5, 17, 21, 23.

3 Find all the factors of 16. Show your workings, so that it is clear you found them all.

B Number patterns, sequences and generalisations

1 What are the next three terms of this sequence: 351, 326, 301…? What is the rule that generates this sequence?

2 When two numbers are added together, the answer is odd. What does this mean about the two numbers?

3 Will the answer be odd or even? Use what you know about the result of multiplying odd and even numbers. You do not need to calculate.

   a 134×17 b 245×19 c 238×24 d $134 \times 2 \times 2$ e $245 \times 2 \times 2$

C Multiplication and division

Work out these multiplication and division calculations.

1 a 91×22 b 45×16 c 27×8 d 276×6 e 4276×6

2 a $49 \div 2$ b $83 \div 9$ c $362 \div 9$ d $475 \div 25$ e $\$5.60 \div 7$

3 Find the missing digits in these calculations. Write down the three calculations.

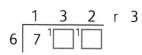

4

> 478   632
>   350
> 725   580

Use what you know about tests of divisibility to help answer these questions.

a Which of these numbers are exactly divisible by 4?

b Which of these numbers are exactly divisible by 25?

9a Handling data

Explore

Here are the results of a cross-country race between Nita's school, Star School, and a visiting school, Eco School.

Position	Time	School
1	12:52	Eco
2	13:01	Star
3	13:02	Eco
4	13:04	Star
5	13:09	Star
6	13:15	Star
7	13:40	Star
8	14:04	Eco
9	14:04	Star
10	14:06	Star
11	14:07	Star
12	14:10	Eco
13	14:10	Star
14	14:17	Eco
15	14:20	Star
16	14:25	Star
17	14:25	Star
18	14:39	Star
19	14:58	Star
20	15:02	Star

Position	Time	School
21	15:02	Eco
22	15:07	Star
23	15:20	Eco
24	15:21	Eco
25	15:23	Eco
26	15:23	Eco
27	15:29	Eco
28	15:38	Eco
29	15:51	Eco
30	16:01	Eco
31	16:05	Star
32	16:05	Star
33	16:17	Eco
34	16:31	Eco
35	16:47	Eco
36	16:53	Eco
37	16:58	Star
38	17:02	Star
39	17:23	Eco
40	19:47	Eco

A runner from Eco School won the race in 12 minutes and 52 seconds, but Nita thinks that the runners in Star School did better overall. What could Nita do to prove or disprove this idea?

Key words

bar chart

average

mode

median

mean

Using a bar chart to test an idea

Learn

Nita decided to count how many runners from her school finished in each position of the race. This is the chart she made.

Runner position	Tally	Number of runners from Star School
1st to 10th	卌 II	7
11th to 20th	卌 III	8
21th to 30th	I	1
31st to 40th	IIII	4

Then Nita turned her frequency chart into a bar chart.

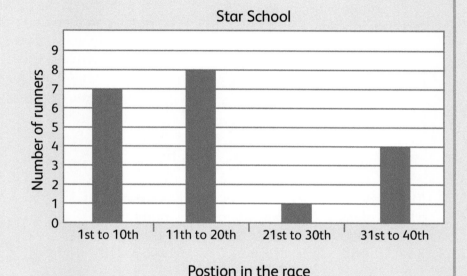

Star School

Does Nita's chart help to see the results? What else needs to be done to test Nita's idea?

Practise

1 Make a frequency chart like Nita's, but for the runners from Eco School.

2 Use the data from your frequency chart to make a bar chart like Nita's.

3 Compare your chart with Nita's. Nita's conjecture was that runners from Star School were faster on average, even though Eco School won the race. Explain whether you think the charts confirm or disprove Nita's idea.

Think like a mathematician

Nita's idea is what mathematicians call a 'conjecture'. This is a statement that needs to be tested to find out whether it is sometimes, always, or never true.

Three averages: Mean, median and mode

Learn

The owner of a sports shop wants to find out which sizes of running shoe sell best. Here are the sizes the shop sold recently:

Kind of running shoe	Sizes sold
Men's shoes	40, 47, 40, 46, 43, 40, 40, 44, 40, 38
Women's shoes	35, 39, 30, 33, 37, 35, 36, 35, 34, 35

How can the owner use the data to decide which shoe sizes sell best?

The mode is the most common value. For the men's shoes it was 40.

The median is the middle value. Put all the items in order, and then find the one (or two) in the middle. If there are values in the middle, the median is halfway between them. For the men, the two middle values are 40 and 40, so the median value is 40.

The mean is an average calculated by adding up all the values and then dividing by the number of values. For the men's shoes this is:
$38 + 40 + 40 + 40 + 40 + 40 + 43 + 44 + 46 = 418$
$418 \div 10 = 41.8$

The range is the difference between the largest and smallest values. For the men's shoes this is: $47 - 38 = 9$.

How can you find the median if there is an even number of items?

Practise

1 Calculate the following for the women's shoes:

   a Mode

   b Median

   c Mean

   d Range.

2 Carry out a survey about shoe sizes in your class.
   Find the mode, median, mean and range of your data.

I think the girls will have a larger range than the boys.

Drawing a line graph

Learn

Kim and Caleb are on a cycle trip. They are recording the distance they travel on tracking devices. Here is the data for Kim.

Time	Total distance travelled
9.00	0 km
10.00	8 km
11.00	15 km
12.00	17.5 km
13.00	17.5 km
14.00	22 km
15.00	30 km

When Kim returns home, she plots her journey on a graph.

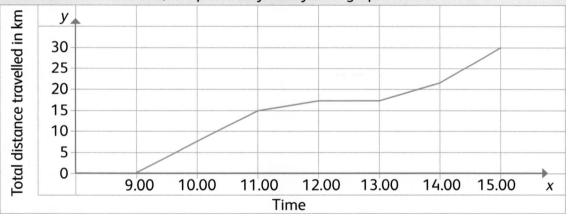

In which hour did she travel the furthest?

Why is the graph horizontal between 12.00 and 13.00? What could explain this?

Practise

1 Here is the tracking data for Caleb.

Time	Total distance travelled
9.00	0 km
10.00	10 km
11.00	16 km
12.00	19.5 km
13.00	22 km
14.00	22 km
15.00	24.5 km

1 Draw a line graph to show the distance Caleb covered.

2 a Which cyclist travelled the furthest?

   b How far did each cyclist travel between 11.a.m. and 1 p.m.?

Converting currencies

Learn

This graph shows the exchange rate between $ and £.

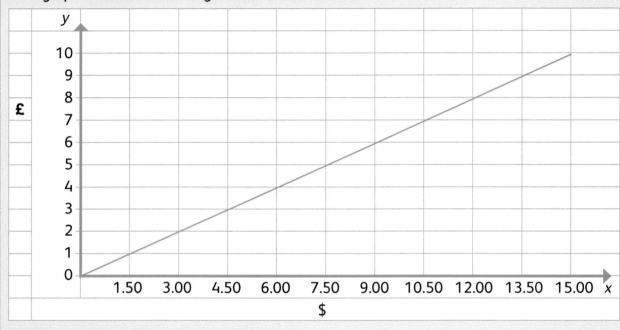

How much would £3 be worth in dollars?

Approximately how much would $5 be in pounds?

Practise

1 Copy and complete the table to show the conversions.

£	$
1	
	3
4	
7	
	15

2 Choose reasonable approximations for the following:

a $4 is approximately £?

b $11 is approximately £?

c £2.50 is approximately $?

d £7.50 is approximately $?

e $12.75 is approximately £?

Try this

Discuss with your partner how you could use the information to work out how to exchange £100 for dollars, or $100 for pounds.

9b Probability

Explore

1. I think it is likely to rain.
2. The probability of sunshine is almost certain.
3. It is likely we will have snow later in the year.
4. The chances of a strong wind are unlikely.
5. Rain here is impossible.

Which speech bubbles could apply to the different climates?

Can you invent some of your own statements using these words.

possible   probably   likely   unlikely   certain   impossible   chances

This bus has been late every day this week.

I suppose it's very likely it will be late today then.

How can people work out what is likely to happen?

Key words
certain
likely
unlikely
impossible
probability
event

The language of probability

While we can use words such as 'unlikely' and 'probable', we can also use percentages to describe probability more accurately.

Which percentages describe the probability of landing on:

a   a blue shape?   b   a red shape?

c   a circle?   d   a star?

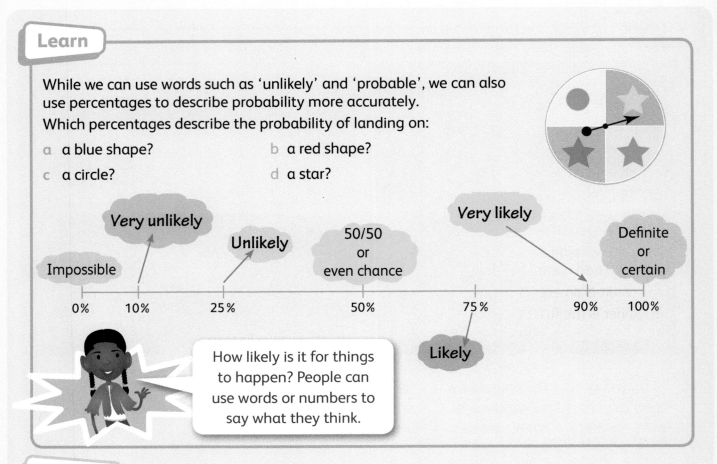

How likely is it for things to happen? People can use words or numbers to say what they think.

1   Decide whether you think these events are certain, likely, even, unlikely or impossible. Also give a percentage as an estimate for the probability.

   a   The sun will rise tomorrow.   b   Mateo's dad's lottery ticket will win the big prize.

   c   A dolphin on a bicycle will eat your maths book.

   d   You toss a coin and get 'heads'.

2   What is the probability of spinning:

   a   a yellow shape?   b   a red shape?

   c   a shape that is not a circle?   d   a shape with fewer than 5 corners?

Choose the best option from these words: impossible, unlikely, even chance, very likely or certain. Also give your answers as percentages for the probability.

3 Thandi has to pick one of Caleb's cards.
   Use the language of probability to describe Thandi's chances of picking the following cards:

   a A card with a triangle

   b A card with a 2-D shape

   c A card that does NOT have a four-sided shape

   d A card with a hexagon.

   Now give each answer as a percentage.

Try this

Play this game for two people. Before you start, choose one person to be Player A and one person to be Player B.

Spin two 1–6 spinners and multiply the two scores. If the result is an odd number, Player A wins a point.

If the result is an even number, Player B wins a point.

The winner is the first to get ten points.

Player	Score
Player A	卌
Player B	‖

I am Player A so I win a point.

There are the same number of odds and evens on the spinner, so there should be 50 % chance of winning.

Do you agree with Mateo?

Invent new rules that are more fair for this game. Try these:

● Player A scores a point if the total is more than …

● Player A scores a point if the difference between the two numbers is …

Think like a mathematician

If probabilities are based on good mathematics, they are not just guesses about the future. But probability cannot tell you exactly what is going to happen, only what is likely. An event that is very unlikely is not impossible, so it might still happen!

9c Data handling and probability problems

Explore

What different data could you collect about these trees?

What questions could you answer by collecting data about the trees?

Solving probability problems

Learn

Scientists are exploring the habitat to discover different species that live there.

The diver makes 10 trips, and collects 10 specimens each time.

The scientists record their findings in a chart.

Trips	Types of sea animals				
	Sea snail	Clownfish	Starfish	Lobster	TOTAL
1	JHT I	III	I		JHT JHT
2	JHT	IIII	I		JHT JHT
3	JHT	III	II		JHT JHT
4	JHT II	II		I	JHT JHT
5	JHT I	III	I		JHT JHT
6	JHT II	II	I		JHT JHT
7	JHT I	III	I		JHT JHT
8	JHT II	II	I		JHT JHT
9	JHT	IIII	I		JHT JHT
10	JHT II	II	I		JHT JHT

Calculate the mean number of sea snails found per trip.

Is the mean greater or less than the median?

Practise

1 Make a chart to show how many different kinds of sea animals have been found.

2 Calculate the mean and the median for the number of clownfish, starfish and lobsters found per dive.

3 Use the information to calculate the probability of finding:

   a a snail

   b a clownfish

   c a starfish

   d a lobster.

   Write the probability as a percentage.

Try this

Choose one of the following to investigate by collecting information from your class:

a Number of brothers and sisters (siblings) learners have

b Mode of travel to school

c The mean length of words from a class book. Choose a page at random from a book, and collect information about 50 words.

Discuss the best way to organise your investigation with a partner.

Tally chart

Mode of transport	Number of learners
cycle	IIII
walk	JHt IIII
car	II
bus	III
other	I

Frequency table

Word length	Frequency
two letters or less	5
three letters	21
four letters	13
five letters	5
six letters or more	6

mode

The range is 2 to 6 letters
The median is 3 letters
The mode is 3 letters

Bar graph

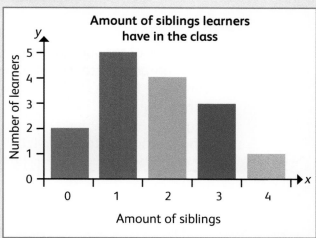

Amount of siblings learners have in the class

121

Self-check

A Handling data

1 The number of passengers using a bus service was recorded each day for ten days. Here are the results:

Day	Number of passengers
1	497
2	501
3	505
4	478
5	509
6	512
7	501
8	511
9	499
10	501

Work out the median, mode, mean and range. Give your answers to the nearest whole number.

B Probability

1 The students in a class discuss their favourite fruit.

Favourite fruit	Number of children
Banana	5
Pineapple	2
Orange	2
Lychee	1

A child is chosen at random to bring their favourite fruit to school. Use the language of probability to describe the chances that the fruit…
a is a banana
b is a lychee
c is an egg
d has a name that contains the letter 'a'.

Unit 10 Problem solving and review

10a Problem solving

Explore

The Olympic Games take place in Nita and Mateo's home town this year!
If a stadium holds 55 000 people and a bus takes 55 people, how many buses do you think will be needed to transport the people to the stadium?

Challenge 1

Nita, Mateo and their classmates fill up three buses to go on a tour of the Olympic Villages.

The tour usually takes 1 hour and spends an equal amount of time in each village. However, on Tuesday there were many unexpected events.

START
13:30

Village A
The red bus had a flat tyre. The trip took six times as long.

Village C
The buses split up, and so could go through the village in a third of the time.

Village E
A surprise visit from a celebrity athlete added 26 minutes to the travel time.

Village B
No traffic, so made up eight minutes of travel time.

Village D
A long line at the tourist shop caused a 15-minute delay.

1 How much longer did the tour take on Tuesday?

2 At what time did the learners get back from the tour?

3 How long would the yellow bus take if it did not wait for the red bus to have its tyre changed?

Challenge 2

There were Olympic Games in Ancient Greece from 776 BCE to 393 CE. In 1896, the modern Olympic Games started as a way of bringing athletes from different countries together. Modern Olympics have been held in (or are planned for) these years:

1896, 1900, 1904, 1908, 1912, 1920, 1924, 1928, 1932, 1936, 1948, 1952, 1956, 1960, 1964, 1968, 1972, 1976, 1980, 1984, 1988, 1992, 1996, 2000, 2004, 2008, 2012, 2016, 2020, 2024, 2028, 2032 …

1 How many years are there between each Olympic Games? Have there been any years where the Games should have been held, but weren't?

2 If the modern Olympic Games continue, in what year will they have been going on for longer than the Ancient Greek Olympics?

Challenge 3

The winners of each event will stand on a winners' platform, called a podium, to get their medals. Caleb and Kim help to make the podium.

This is the podium's measurements: The front of the podium is a piece of wood like this:

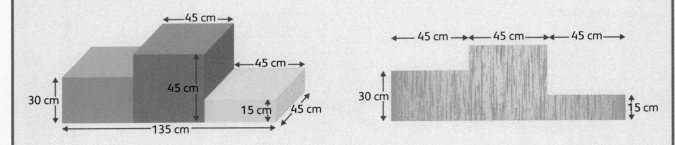

1 The front of the podium is cut from a sheet of wood that measures 135 cm × 45 cm. What is the area of this sheet?

2 What is the area of the finished podium front?

3 Kim wants to put gold ribbon around the base of this shape. How much ribbon will she need?

4 How can you use the area of the front sheet to calculate the area of the whole podium? Explain how you reached this result.

Challenge 4

1 Hiram decides to practise his long jump. The table shows the results of his jumps.

Practice session	Best jump (m)
1	2.76
2	2.89
3	2.80
4	2.93
5	2.95

a How much further than his first practice jump can Hiram jump after five practice jumps?

b Do you think Hiram is improving quickly enough to be able to jump more than 300 cm in time for the competition? How could you estimate how soon he would be able to jump that far? What are some of the difficulties in making these kinds of estimates?

c What is the median of his jumps?

d Hiram jumps a final jump of 3.67 m. What is the mean of his jumps?

Challenge 5

Star School had an Olympic-style sports competition. Two other schools, Eco School and Hope School, also took part. The event organisers lost the sheet with the results of the girls' 800 m race in minutes and seconds. Kim and Thandi draw it up from what they remember.

Place	Name	Time	School
1st		5.01	Hope
2nd			Star
3rd		5.03	Eco
4th	Jasmine		Hope
5th		5.07	Eco
6th	Thandi	5.11	Star
7th	Sara		Eco
8th	Kim	5.17	Star
9th		5.19	Hope
10th			Star

1 Copy and complete the race information table. Use these clues to work out the missing information.

- Maria and Jasmine's times had a difference of only two seconds between them.
- Jasmine's time was the mean of Maria's and Lin's times.
- Lin was the best runner from Eco school.
- Elena came either first or last.
- Nita came second or second last.
- There is a difference of 4 seconds between Miriam and Aisha's race times.
- Miriam's position in the race was a multiple of Lin's position.
- The total of Thandi's, Elena's and Miriam's race times is 15.25.

2 Kim noticed something very interesting about the race times. What is it?

3 If the race times follow the sequence, what time would the 15th runner have?

125

Challenge 6

Use the table of information about Olympic athletes to answer the questions below.

Athlete	Height (cm)	Weight (kg)	Woman (W) or man (M)?	Sport/ Martial art
A	136	30	W	Gymnastics
B	140	62	W	Weightlifting
C	141	35	W	Gymnastics
D	149	35	W	Gymnastics
E	185	75	M	Judo
F	186	125	M	Weightlifting
G	208	160	M	Shot-put
H	212	102	M	Basketball
I	212	115	M	Basketball
J	219	110	M	Basketball

1   How has this table been arranged?

2   Two of the athletes are in a lift. When one gets out, the weight in the lift exactly halves. Another athlete gets into the lift. Now the weight in the lift is 145 kg. Who is in the lift now?

3   a   What is the height and weight of the average athlete in this group?

   b   How do the weights and heights of the basketball players differ from those of the weightlifters? (Think about the mean, median and range.)

   c   If an athlete has a height of 165 cm and a weight of 55 kg, would he or she be a weightlifter or a gymnast? How do you know?

   d   Make a hypothesis about the weight and height of athletes in each sport. Discuss which strategies you could use to test and refine your hypothesis.

4   One of these Olympic athletes was chosen at random to open the Olympic-style school sports competition. How likely is it that:

   a   the athlete is a man?

   b   the athlete is Nita's hero, athlete D?

Unit 11 Number and problem solving

11a Place value and decimal numbers

Explore

Tea $1.25   Coffee $1.40   Hot chocolate $1.75
Hot drinks

Key words

exact
conversions

A man buys hot drinks for himself and nine friends.
What is the most he can spend on ten drinks?
What is the least he can spend on ten drinks?
Can he spend exactly $13 on ten drinks?

Multiplication and division of decimals with rounding

Learn

I multiplied my number by 10 and rounded it to the nearest whole number. It rounds to 23.

237

24.2

2.34

I divided my number by 100 and rounded it to the nearest tenth. It rounds to 2.4.

What number did each child use? How do you know?

Thousands	Hundreds	Tens	Units	Tenths	Hundredths
	2	3	7		

Now make up a similar problem for ×100 and ÷10 using these numbers.

127

Practise

1 a Complete the calculations.

5.9 × 10	4.45 × 100	1.23 × 10
10 × 5.90	44.5 × 10	12.3 × 10
0.59 × 10	44.5 ÷ 10	123 ÷ 100
5.9 ÷ 10	445 ÷ 100	12.3 ÷ 10

  b Round each of your answers to the blue calculations to the nearest whole number.

  c Round each of your answers to the red calculations to the nearest tenth.

2 Mateo has been finding out about the population of different cities.

City	A	B	C	D	E
Population	1.82 million	1.31 million	1.44 million	1.29 million	1.95 million

He has made a bar chart showing each population rounded to the nearest tenth of a million.

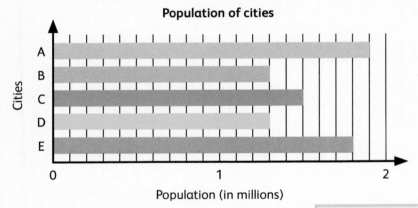

Population of cities

Cities: A, B, C, D, E

Population (in millions)

  a Check Mateo's work. Explain any errors he has made.

  b Nita says that Cities B and D should not have bars of the same length on the chart. Why is Nita wrong?

Try this

A newspaper reports that 38.2 cm of snow fell on one day in December. The actual measurement was rounded to the nearest tenth of a centimetre.

What is the least amount of snow that could have fallen that day?

☐ ☐ . ☐ ☐ cm

Think like a mathematician

When you are asked to give a rounded answer, first write down the **exact** answer and then round it. For example: 991 ÷ 100 = 9.91, which is 9.9 to the nearest tenth.

Comparing and ordering numbers

Learn

| 575 273 | 64 502 | 575 318 | 6 450.28 |

Look carefully at the numbers. What is the same and what is different about them?

6 450.28 and 575 373 have the same number of digits. Which is larger? Why?

The number 64 502 starts with the digit 6, but it is smaller than the number 575 273, which starts with the digit 5. Why?

Two numbers start with the same three digits. How will you decide which number is larger?

Now order the four numbers from smallest to largest.

⬭ < ⬭ < ⬭ < ⬭

Practise

1 Order each set of numbers from smallest to largest.

a 23.4   234   2.34   3.42   b 234 780   32 478   234 799   3 247.8

c 0.25   1.2   0.53   2.1   2.02   d 100 001   10 001   101 001   11 010

2 Use the digits 2, 3, 4 and 5 each time to make these statements correct.

a 46.☐☐ cm < ☐2.☐7 cm   b ☐☐.3 kg > 9.☐☐ kg

c 5.☐ ℓ > ☐.7 ℓ > ☐.☐ ℓ

3 Nita and Mateo place four decimal numbers in order on a number line. They explain how they know where two of the numbers will sit.

a Which two numbers on the number line are the children talking about? Give the letter and the actual number each time.

b Which numbers are shown by the other letters on the number line?

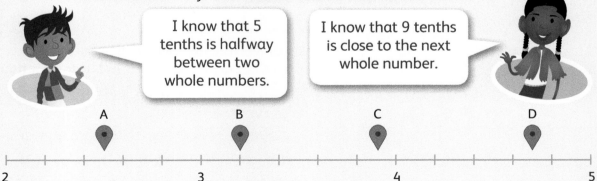

I know that 5 tenths is halfway between two whole numbers.

I know that 9 tenths is close to the next whole number.

Ordering and comparing positive and negative numbers

Learn

Our number system uses positive and negative numbers. Positive numbers get larger as they get further away from zero. What happens to negative numbers as they move further away from zero?

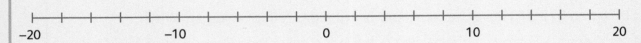

Which number is closer to zero: −18 or 20? Why?

Where will −5 and −9 sit on this number line? Which number is smaller? How much smaller?

Both −16 and 16 are the same distance from zero. Where will they sit on this number line?

Choose another negative number between 0 and −20. Explain where it sits on this number line.

Practise

1 Which numbers do the labels A, B, C, D and E represent on each number line?

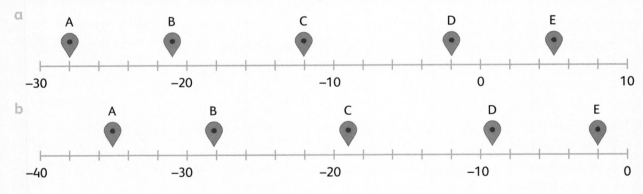

2 Order the temperatures from coldest to hottest.

a −8°C 8°C 0°C −4°C

b 25°C 17.5°C −17.5°C −12°C

c 21°C −12°C 1°C −14°C −20°C

d −3°C −13°C −3.5°C 3°C

Try this

Nita orders four numbers on a number line. All numbers are larger than −20 but smaller than 5.

The smallest number is 15 less than the largest number.

Two numbers are an equal distance from zero.

One of Nita's four numbers is −8.

What could Nita's numbers be? Find at least two possible solutions.

Decimals in litres, kilometres and kilograms

Learn

1 000 grams (g) = 1 kilogram (kg), so every gram (1 g) is $\frac{1}{1000}$ of a kilogram.

You can write 1 g as 0.001 kg.

A mass in grams can therefore be converted into kilograms by dividing by 1 000. For example: 750 g ÷ 1 000 = 0.75 kg

How can a mass in kilograms, for example 3.5 kg, be converted into grams?

Look at these equivalents for length and capacity.

1 000 metres (m) = 1 kilometre (km), so 1 m is $\frac{1}{1000}$ of a kilometre. (1 m = 0.001 km).

1 000 millilitres (ml) = 1 litre (ℓ), so 1 ml is $\frac{1}{1000}$ of a litre (1 ml = 0.001 ℓ).

How can 750 m be converted into kilometres?
How can 3.5 ℓ be converted into millilitres?

Practise

1   Give the correct measurement for each point labelled A–E.
    Write the measurement in litres and then in millilitres.

2   Use the 'greater than' (>), 'less than' (<) or 'equals' (=) signs to compare
    these pairs of measurements. The first one has been done for you.

a   0.75 km and 800 m   0.75 km < 800 m

b   0.060 ℓ and 100 ml   c   1.2 km and 1 200 m

d   500 g and 0.050 kg   e   300 g and 0.3 kg   f   100 ℓ and 100 ml

Try this

Thandi decides to weigh her pet rabbit.
She puts it on a see-saw and uses these
things to balance it. How much does the
rabbit weigh?

● 4 cartons of juice are equal in mass to
  the bag of rice.

● 2 bags of carrots are equal in mass to
  the bag of rice.

● 1 carton of juice has a mass of 0.25 kg.

11b Fractions

Explore

There are 100 symbols in the whole picture. Each symbol represents $\frac{1}{100}$ of the whole. There are 10 rows of symbols. Each row represents $\frac{1}{10}$ of the whole.

How many tenths are equivalent to one whole?
How many tenths are equivalent to half of the whole?

What other equivalent fractions can you make?

Comparing fractions

Learn

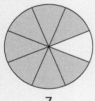 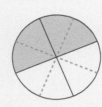 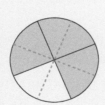 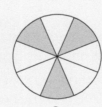 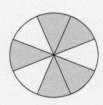 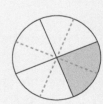

$$\frac{7}{8} \qquad \frac{1}{2} \qquad \frac{3}{4} \qquad \frac{3}{8} \qquad \frac{5}{8} \qquad \frac{1}{4}$$

How can you compare the sizes of fractions?

It's easy to compare fractions that share the same denominator. You can see that $\frac{7}{8} > \frac{3}{8}$ because four more eighths are shaded.

I can use what I know about equivalent fractions to help compare $\frac{1}{4}$ and $\frac{3}{8}$. I can multiply both the numerator and denominator in the fraction $\frac{1}{4}$ by two to give the equivalent fraction $\frac{2}{8}$. Now I can compare $\frac{2}{8}$ and $\frac{3}{8}$ easily.

$\times 2$

$$\frac{1}{4} \qquad \frac{2}{8}$$

$\times 2$

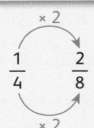 

132

Practise

1 For each pair of fractions, say which one is greater or whether they are equivalent. The first one has been done for you.

a $\frac{2}{4}$ and $\frac{5}{8}$ $\frac{2}{4} = \frac{4}{8}$. So, $\frac{2}{4} < \frac{5}{8}$.

b $\frac{6}{8}$ and $\frac{11}{16}$

c $\frac{3}{10}$ and $\frac{6}{20}$

d $\frac{3}{6}$ and $\frac{2}{3}$

e $\frac{1}{3}$ and $\frac{4}{9}$

f $\frac{1}{3}$ and $\frac{3}{12}$

g $\frac{2}{6}$ and $\frac{3}{12}$

h $\frac{2}{6}$ and $\frac{25}{60}$

i $\frac{1}{9}$ and $\frac{4}{18}$

2 Here are six groups of fractions. Identify the fraction in each group that is not equivalent to the others. The first one has been done for you.

a $\frac{50}{100}$, $\frac{5}{10}$, $\frac{1}{2}$, $\frac{3}{6}$, $\frac{7}{13}$ $\frac{50}{100}$, $\frac{5}{10}$ and $\frac{3}{6}$ are all equivalent to $\frac{1}{2}$.

The fraction that is not equivalent is $\frac{7}{13}$.

b $\frac{5}{15}$, $\frac{1}{3}$, $\frac{3}{10}$, $\frac{6}{18}$

c $\frac{4}{12}$, $\frac{2}{8}$, $\frac{25}{100}$, $\frac{1}{4}$

d $\frac{20}{100}$, $\frac{2}{10}$, $\frac{1}{5}$, $\frac{3}{15}$, $\frac{9}{40}$

e $\frac{7}{8}$, $\frac{75}{100}$, $\frac{9}{12}$, $\frac{6}{8}$, $\frac{3}{4}$

f $\frac{6}{9}$, $\frac{12}{16}$, $\frac{2}{3}$, $\frac{60}{90}$, $\frac{10}{15}$

g $\frac{4}{6}$, $\frac{10}{15}$, $\frac{14}{18}$, $\frac{20}{30}$

Try this

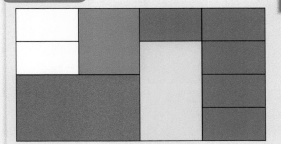

The green sections represent $\frac{5}{16}$ of the whole shape.
Compare the fractions represented by different colours of the whole shape.
Use the symbols <, > and = to show what you have found out.

For example: Blue fraction = white fraction because $\frac{1}{8} = \frac{2}{16}$.

Think like a mathematician

When denominators are different, check to see if one denominator is a multiple of the other. For example, to compare $\frac{3}{5}$ and $\frac{7}{10}$ check to see if 10 is a multiple of 5. It is, so now use your multiplication facts to find how many times larger than 5 it is (5 × 2 = 10).
You must multiply the numerator and denominator by 2 to give the equivalent fraction with denominator 10, so $\frac{3}{5}$ is equivalent to $\frac{6}{10}$, which is smaller than $\frac{7}{10}$.

11c Mixed numbers

Explore

I'm ten and a half.

I'm 10 years and 3 months.

Today's my eleventh birthday!

Stand on the number line to show your age!

7   8   9   10   11   12

Key words

whole number
approximate
difference
negative

Where should the children stand?

Where would you and some friends stand on this number line?

How about a child who is exactly two years younger than you?

Explain how you know.

Mixed numbers and improper fractions

Learn

The fraction $\frac{8}{5}$ is called an improper fraction because the numerator is larger than the denominator. You can say that $\frac{8}{5}$ is equal to $\frac{5}{5} + \frac{3}{5}$ or $1 + \frac{3}{5}$. This can be written using mixed numbers as $1\frac{3}{5}$.

Another strategy is to use what you know about representing a fraction as a division. $\frac{8}{5}$ can be written as $8 \div 5 = 1 \text{ r } 3$ or $1\frac{3}{5}$ as the remainder can be turned into a fraction.

A mixed number has a whole number part and a fraction part.

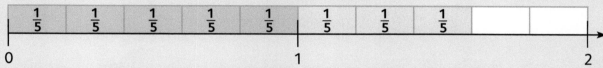

How can you use what you know about the equivalence $\frac{5}{5} = 1$ to help write the mixed number $1\frac{2}{5}$ as an improper fraction?

Practise

1 Convert these improper fractions to mixed numbers.

   a $\frac{8}{6}$ b $\frac{18}{5}$ c $\frac{22}{7}$

   d $\frac{11}{4}$ e $\frac{9}{2}$ f $\frac{10}{2}$

2 Convert these mixed numbers to improper fractions.

   a $5\frac{1}{2}$ b $2\frac{2}{3}$

   c $1\frac{6}{7}$ d $2\frac{6}{7}$

3 Match these numbers to the letters on the number line.

   $1\frac{1}{8}, \quad 2\frac{1}{3}, \quad 4\frac{7}{8}, \quad 6\frac{1}{4}, \quad 8\frac{1}{3}, \quad 9\frac{1}{2}$

Try this

Order the masses of the boxes from lightest to heaviest.

$3\frac{3}{4}$ kg $1\frac{1}{4}$ kg $4\frac{1}{2}$ kg $\frac{18}{8}$ kg $\frac{30}{10}$ kg

Now write a mass that is heavier than all of these?

Give it as a mixed number and an improper fraction.

Think like a mathematician

Remember that every whole can be written as a fraction.

For example: 1 whole = $\frac{2}{2}$ or $\frac{3}{3}$ or $\frac{4}{4}$ or $\frac{5}{5}$ or $\frac{6}{6}$, and so on.

135

⟳ 11d **Equivalences**

Explore

How many people in the whole group are female?
What fraction of the whole group is this?

Which other groups can you find in the picture?

What fraction of the whole group do they represent each time?

Can you give any of these fractions as decimals?

Key words ⟳
simplify
numerator
equivalence

Simplifying fractions

Learn

The fraction $\frac{3}{4}$ is said to be in its simplest form because both the numerator and denominator cannot be divided any further to still leave whole digits.

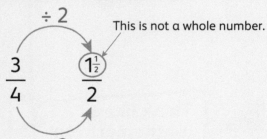

$\div 2$ — This is not a whole number.

$$\frac{3}{4} \quad \frac{1\frac{1}{2}}{2}$$

$\div 2$

However, the fraction $\frac{6}{9}$ is not in its simplest form because both the numerator and denominator can be divided by the same amount to leave whole digits.

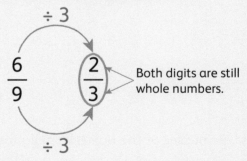

$\div 3$

$$\frac{6}{9} \quad \frac{2}{3}$$ Both digits are still whole numbers.

$\div 3$

The fraction $\frac{6}{9}$ has now been reduced to its simplest form, $\frac{2}{3}$.
You know that it is now in its simplest form because both the numerator and the denominator cannot be divided any further to still leave whole digits.

Practise

1 Which of these fractions are already in their simplest form? Can you explain why?

$\frac{1}{2}$ $\frac{4}{10}$ $\frac{5}{8}$ $\frac{3}{9}$ $\frac{5}{20}$ $\frac{2}{5}$

2 These fractions are equivalent. True or false?

a $\frac{5}{10} = \frac{1}{2}$ b $\frac{15}{25} = \frac{3}{4}$ c $\frac{7}{21} = \frac{1}{4}$ d $\frac{9}{12} = \frac{3}{4}$ e $\frac{18}{54} = \frac{2}{8}$

3 What fraction of each shape is shaded? Write each fraction in its simplest form.

a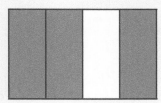

b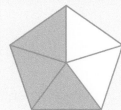

c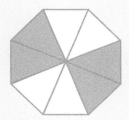

d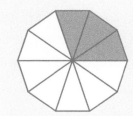

e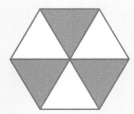

f

Think like a mathematician

A fraction can be simplified when both the numerator and denominator can be found in the same multiplication table.
For example: $\frac{2}{4}$ can be simplified because 2 and 4 are both in the two times table. A fraction with numerator one cannot be simplified.

Converting fractions to decimals

Learn

I have to say what $\frac{7}{25}$ is as a decimal. So I have to do 7 ÷ 25. Where is the calculator?

No, you can use equivalence fractions to help you. Can you find an equivalent fraction with a denominator of 10 or 100?

I can multiply the numerator and denominator by 4 to give the equivalent fraction $\frac{28}{100}$. But how does that help me?

You can do the division just by using place value. $\frac{28}{100}$ means 28 ÷ 100 and that is 0.28.

To convert a fraction into a decimal, you divide the **numerator** by the denominator. You can use **equivalences** to make the division easier. $\frac{2}{5}$ as a decimal is 0.4.

Can you find an equivalent fraction with denominator 10 or 100 to help you check?

You can also convert $\frac{2}{5}$ to a decimal using the calculation 2 ÷ 5.

$$\begin{array}{r} 0\ .\ 4 \\ 5\overline{)\,2\ .\ {}^2 0} \end{array}$$

Practise

1 Convert these fractions to decimal numbers. Remember to first think about finding an equivalent fraction with denominator 10 or 100.

a $\frac{1}{10}$ b $\frac{71}{100}$ c $\frac{1}{5}$ d $\frac{1}{25}$ e $\frac{9}{20}$

2 Write each of these measurements as a decimal.

a $\frac{3}{4}$ kg   b $\frac{4}{5}$ km   c $\frac{9}{10}$ ℓ   d $\frac{3}{8}$ km   e $\frac{5}{8}$ kg

3 a Nita scores $\frac{17}{20}$ in her spelling test. What is this fraction as a decimal?

   b Mateo scores $\frac{21}{25}$ in his spelling test. What is this fraction as a decimal?

   c Who got the largest fraction of their whole test correct? Explain how you know.

Try this

Put these fractions in order from smallest to largest using their decimal equivalents to help you.

$\frac{9}{25}$ $\frac{7}{8}$ $\frac{13}{20}$ $\frac{4}{5}$ $\frac{1}{4}$ $\frac{69}{100}$

11e Addition and subtraction, including decimal numbers

Explore

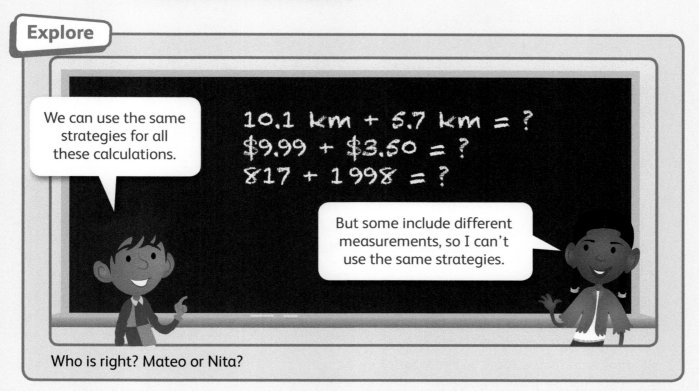

We can use the same strategies for all these calculations.

$$10.1 \text{ km} + 5.7 \text{ km} = ?$$
$$\$9.99 + \$3.50 = ?$$
$$817 + 1998 = ?$$

But some include different measurements, so I can't use the same strategies.

Who is right? Mateo or Nita?

Using number facts and place value

Key words
near multiples
total

Learn

What is the same and what is different about each of these calculations?

| 3 + 7 = 10 | 300 + 700 = 1000 | 0.3 + 0.7 = 1 |

The same number fact 3 + 7 = 10 has been used, but place value changes the size of the calculations.

Now think about the number fact: 18 − 6 = 12
Can you make this calculation 10 times larger? How about 100 times larger?

1.8 − 0.6 = 1.2   How many times smaller is this calculation than the number fact 18 − 6 = 12?

You can check each of these calculations using the inverse.
300 + 700 = 1000 is correct because 1000 − 700 = 300.

Practise

1 Find the missing numbers as quickly as you can.

a 13 + ☐ = 19 b 20 − ☐ = 8 c ☐ = 8 + 5 d 10 + ☐ = 20 − 6

e ☐ − 10 = 7 f ☐ + 13 = 17 g 5 + 11 = ☐ − 4 h 19 − ☐ = 8

2 Complete these calculations. Write the number fact you used each time. The first one has been done for you.

a	b	c	d
0.6 + 0.4 60 + 40 600 + 400	140 − 70 1.4 − 0.7 70 + 70	7.8 + 2.2 780 + 220 0.78 + 0.22	10 − 6.5 1 000 − 650 1 − 0.65
Number fact: 6 + 4 = 10	Number fact:	Number fact:	Number fact:

3 Nita has 45 cents in her pocket and 23 cents in her money box. Mateo has ten times as much money in his pocket as Nita. He also has 10 times as much in his money box.

a How much money does Nita have?

b How much money does Mateo have?

Write the calculation you used.

Try this

Nita's number puzzle:

I'm thinking of an addition number fact ☐ + ☐ = 58.
I divide each number in my calculation by 10 to give
the calculation ☐ + 2.5 = ☐.
I use my number fact again and now multiply each
number by 10. I write the new calculation as a
subtraction using the inverse. ☐ − 250 = ☐

Find:

a the addition number fact that Nita uses each time

b her decimal calculation

c her subtraction calculation.

Adding and subtracting near multiples of 1, 10, 100 or 1 000

Learn

You have used strategies of rounding and adjusting to mentally add or subtract a near multiple of 10, 100 and 1 000 or a near whole unit of money.

Explain to a partner how you would compete these calculations using rounding and adjusting.

| 245 + 39 | 678 – 298 | 4 607 – 1 999 | $35.75 + $2.02 |

You can use the same strategies to add or subtract near multiples of one.
Look at the calculations 4.5 + 1.9 and 4.5 – 1.9

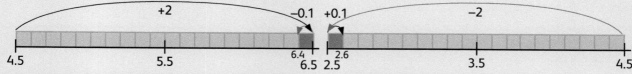

For the calculation 4.5 + 1.9, two wholes have been added but this is 0.1 too much.
For the calculation 4.5 –1.9, two wholes have been subtracted but again this is 0.1 too much.
Can you explain what must happen next?

Practise

1 Complete these calculations using a rounding and adjusting strategy.
   Explain why this method is easier than using a written method for these calculations.

a	b	c	d
467 + 29	567 + 298	6 675 + 2 997	$66.75 + $29.97
467 – 29	567 – 98	6 675 – 2 997	$66.75 – $29.97
4.6 + 3.1	567 –102	6 675 + 3 003	$66.75 – $30.03

2 Say whether these calculations are true or false? Correct any calculations that are false.

   a 5.6 + 2.9 = 8.6   b 5.6 – 1.9 = 3.7   c 7.4 + 3.8 = 11.2   d 7.4 – 3.1 = 4.5

   e Use the inverse to prove that 6.3 – 1.9 = 4.2 is not true.

3 The table shows the amount of rainfall in the morning and afternoon during a week.

	Monday	Tuesday	Wednesday	Thursday	Friday
am	6.5 mm	8.2 mm	7.4 mm	9.3 mm	12.7 mm
pm	2.9 mm	3.9 mm	2.1 mm	3.2 mm	4.8 mm

   a Calculate the total rainfall for each day.

   b What is the difference between the amount of rainfall in the morning and afternoon on Monday?

   c The rainfall in the morning on one of the days was 5.3 mm more than in the afternoon.
      Which day was this?

   d What was the largest difference between the morning and afternoon rainfall on the same
      day? Which day was this?

Try this

Use each number once to complete these calculations correctly.

| 3.2 | 2.5 | 2.8 | 8.3 | 7.4 |

$5.2 + 3.9 - \boxed{} = 6.3$

$\boxed{} + 3.2 + 1.7 = \boxed{}$

$\boxed{} - 1.6 + \boxed{} = 9.9$

Think like a mathematician

Remember to think carefully about how you need to adjust your calculations each time. Have you added or subtracted too much or not enough?

Using addition and subtraction

Learn

The table shows the number and total costs of newspapers and comics sold in one day at four different shops.

	Number of newspapers sold	Total cost of newspapers sold	Number of comics sold	Total cost of comics sold
Shop A	67	$50.35	78	$58.50
Shop B	135	$101.90	49	$44.35
Shop C	84	$66.36	163	$133.60
Shop D	152	$120.08	204	$178.20

What is an appropriate method to use to find the total number of newspapers sold on that day? And what is an appropriate method to find the total cost?

Can you make a useful estimation for each calculation?

Will the actual answers be greater or less than your estimates?

Here a written method is used for each calculation.

```
 H T U              $
   6 7            5 0 . 3 5
   8 4            6 6 . 3 6
 1 3 5          1 0 1 . 9 0
+1 5 2         +1 2 0 . 0 8
```

Complete the calculations.

Does it matter that the order of the numbers in the calculations above is not the same order shown in the table?

Practise

1 Use the table in the *Learn* activity to work out these calculations. Remember to make an estimate first.

   a The total number of comics sold that day

   b The total cost of the comics sold that day.

   c Check that your answer to part a) is correct by adding the numbers in a different order.

2 Nita goes on a walk and makes a rough measure of the distance by counting her strides.

Part of the journey	Number of strides
To the park	97
From the park to the market	185
Across the market	93
To Grandmother's house	92

   a Don't calculate the total yet – make an estimate. Will your estimate be greater or less than the exact answer?

   b What is the exact answer? Show your working and be ready to explain why you chose the method you used.

   c If Nita's stride is about half a metre, how far did she walk?

3 Complete these calculations. Remember to make an estimate first.

   a $35.6 - 12.5$ b $35.6 + 12.5 + 2.4$ c $75.25 - 31.18$ d $75.25 + 31.18$

   e Check your answers using the inverse. Write the calculation you use each time.

Try this

Find the value of the different coloured bars using the bar model clues to help you.

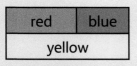

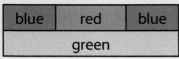

Think like a mathematician

For *Try this*, look for the most useful starting point. Remember that it may not be the first bar model clue.

Finding the difference

Learn

Remember that the difference between two numbers can be found by comparing the two numbers and finding out how much more or less one number is than the other.

For example, the difference between 2 523 and 2 375 is 148.

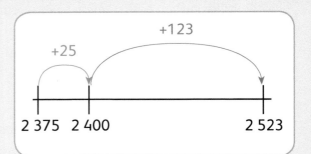

You can use this method to find the difference between positive and negative numbers.

Use this number line to find the difference between −8 and 10.

It is always useful to stop at zero when counting from negative to positive numbers or vice versa.

Now find the difference between −8 and −10.

Explain why the difference is much smaller this time.

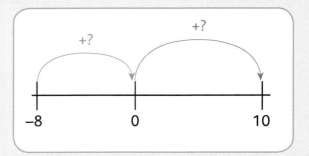

Practise

1 Find the difference between the pairs of numbers each time. Sketch a number line to help you.

   a 12 and −12   b −2 and −12   c 20 and −1   d −1 and 20   e −1 and −20

2 How much colder is:

   a −5 °C than 7 °C?   b −18 °C than 0 °C?   c −19 °C than −1 °C?   d −13 °C than 15 °C?

3 Complete the following statements to make them true.

   a ☐ °C is 10° warmer than −2 °C.

   b −14 °C is ☐° colder than 6 °C.

   c −3 °C is 17° warmer than ☐ °C.

Think like a mathematician

Remember to stop at zero to help you. Also think about using your number facts to 20 to help you calculate.

Self-check

A Place value and decimal numbers

1 Do these calculations and give your answer to the nearest tenth.
   a $12.159 \times 10 =$
   b $1.151 \times 10 =$
   c $1\,875 \div 100 =$

2 A restaurant bill for ten friends comes to $182.78.
   The friends decide to round the bill to the nearest $100 so they can leave a tip.
   a What is the rounded amount?
   b How much should they each pay to share the cost equally?

3 If these numbers were put on a number line, which two would be closest together?
   Sketch a number line if you find it helpful.
   0.19, 0.91, 0.199

4 Which is further, 1.297 km or 197.29 metres?

B Fractions

1 Find the value of ★ to make these statements correct.
   a $\dfrac{★}{4} = \dfrac{9}{12}$ b $\dfrac{9}{10} = \dfrac{★}{100}$

   c $\dfrac{3}{4} < \dfrac{★}{8}$ d $\dfrac{★}{2} > \dfrac{40}{100}$

C Mixed numbers

1 Are the following statements true or false?
   a $\dfrac{13}{15} = 1\dfrac{2}{13}$ b $2\dfrac{2}{3} = \dfrac{8}{3}$ c $\dfrac{15}{7} = 2\dfrac{1}{7}$

   d $10\dfrac{1}{10} = \dfrac{101}{10}$ e $2\dfrac{3}{4}$ is smaller than $3\dfrac{2}{4}$ f $7\dfrac{1}{8}$ is bigger than $8\dfrac{1}{7}$

D Equivalences

1 Can these fractions be simplified, or is the denominator already as small as it can be?
   Simplify them if they are not in their simplest form.

   a $\dfrac{2}{4}$ b $\dfrac{6}{24}$ c $\dfrac{1}{9}$

2 Convert these fractions to decimal numbers.

   a $\dfrac{7}{10}$ b $\dfrac{22}{100}$ c $\dfrac{3}{5}$

E Addition and subtraction including decimal numbers

1 Do these calculations.
   a $170 + 30$ b $3.8 + 6.2$
   c $15.6 + 1.7$ d $\$1.38 + \$2.62$
   e $2\,507 - 1\,998$

Unit 12 Measures and problem solving

⏻ 12a The metric system

Explore

This family has made a mistake with their volleyball court. Can you figure out what has happened?

Can you work out the total area of the family's volleyball court?

What about the perimeter?

Can you estimate the measurements for other types of sport, for example: a football pitch, a tennis court, a chessboard, and so on. Try giving the estimates in both metric and imperial units.

Key words

pound
pint
ounce
gallon

Converting measures

Learn

Write 0.01 km in metres.

To convert kilometres, you divide by 1 000.

Write 1.1 m in centimetres.

1.1 m is 1 m 1 cm, which is 101 cm.

Both children have made a mistake. Can you spot the errors and find the correct conversions?

Practise

1 Convert these measurements. Your answers should all be whole numbers.

   a Convert 1.25 kg to grams.   b Convert 2.25 litres to millilitres.

   c Convert 3.25 km to metres.   d Convert 0.125 kg to grams.

   e Convert 0.005 kg to grams.   f Convert 0.01 litres to millilitres.

   g Convert 0.01 metres to centimetres.   h Convert 0.01 km to metres.

2 How much do the cat and the mouse weigh? Give your answer in grams and kilograms.

35.6 kg

39.47 kg

39.513 kg

3 Mateo pours 50 ml into each container.
Write the number of litres in each container now.
Then Nita adds 99 ml into each jug.
Write the total volume of all four jugs in litres.

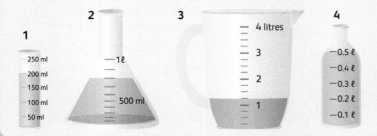

Try this

1 metre (approximately) = 3 feet and 3 inches

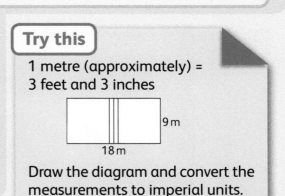

9 m

18 m

Draw the diagram and convert the measurements to imperial units.

Imperial units for weight and volume

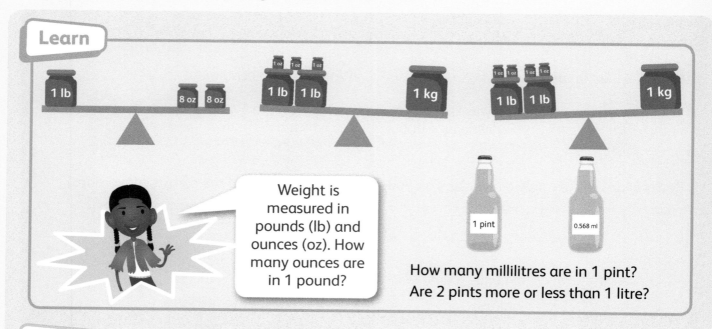

Weight is measured in pounds (lb) and ounces (oz). How many ounces are in 1 pound?

How many millilitres are in 1 pint?
Are 2 pints more or less than 1 litre?

Practise

1 Which is the greater amount?

  a 25 lb or 10 kg

  b 1 gallon (= 8 pints) or 10 ℓ

  c 3 kg or 6 lb

  d 37 lb or 16 kg

  e 10 gallons (= 80 pints) or 50 ℓ

2 a How many ounces are in 5 pounds?

  b Approximately how many pounds are in 2 kilograms?

  c Approximately how many pounds are in 10 kilograms?

3 A trolley has a weight limit of 200 lb.

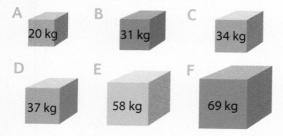

Look at boxes A to F.

a Can Box F go on the trolley?

b Which box can be carried with Box E on the trolley?

c Find two groups of 3 boxes that can be carried together.

4 American recipes sometimes use a measurement called a 'cup'. 1 cup = $\frac{1}{2}$ pint. A gō is a traditional Japanese measure. 1 gō = 180 ml. Is a gō greater than or less than 1 cup?

Think like a mathematician

To check your conversions between metric and imperial, think about whether you expect your answer to be a bigger or smaller number than you started with. For example, one litre is more than one pint, so if you convert litres to pints, your answer should be a larger number.

12b Length, area and perimeter

Explore

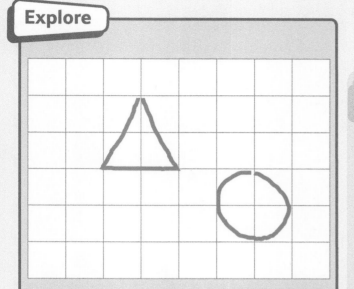

The same loop of string is used to make two different shapes.

Which shape has the largest area?

Length, area and perimeter

Learn

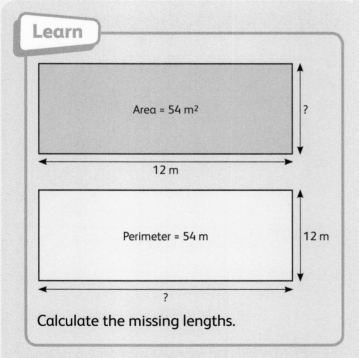

Calculate the missing lengths.

Practise

1 Here are the measurements of some rectangles. Work out the area and perimeter of each one.

   a 30 cm × 50 cm   b 24 cm × 4 cm
   c 20 cm × 10 cm   d 90 m × 30 m
   e 16 mm × 3 mm

2 Mateo wants to make a poster measuring 90 cm × 61 cm. He will need to tape together pieces of paper, each measuring 30 cm × 21 cm. He wants to use as few pieces of paper as possible. How many pieces does he need? How long a ribbon will he need to make a border for the poster?

3 Work out the missing lengths for each shape.

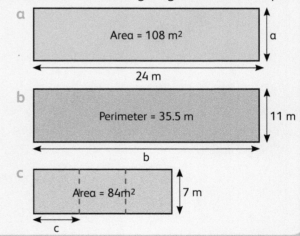

Try this

A 3 cm × 6 cm rectangle has a perimeter of 18 cm and an area of 18 cm². How would you find out whether there are any other rectangles where the perimeter and area are the same number?

12c Time

Explore

Estimate how long it takes to complete each event shown in the photographs A to E.

Research the world record for the quickest times or longest matches.

Does a tennis ball travel faster than a racing car? How could you measure the speed of each one?

Key words

clock

duration

month

departure and arrival times

Solving problems about time

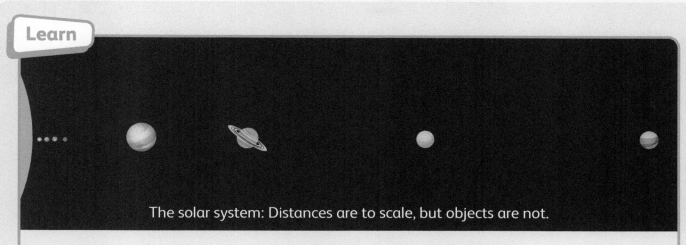

The solar system: Distances are to scale, but objects are not.

The distance from the Earth to the sun is called 1 AU (Astronomical Unit).

It takes light 8 minutes to travel from the sun to Earth (approximately 150 million km).

How far would light travel in four minutes?

Practise

1 a How far could light travel in one hour?

   b What calculations would tell you how far light can travel in a day?

   c Write an approximation for how far light would travel in a week.

2

Planet	Distance (approximate)	Time for light from the sun to reach planet
Mercury	$\frac{1}{2}$ AU	a
Earth	1 AU	8 minutes
Mars	$1\frac{1}{2}$ AU	b
Jupiter	5 AU	c
Saturn	d	1 hour 20 minutes
Uranus	e	160 minutes
Neptune	30 AU	f

Copy and complete the table.

Try this

Use the information in the table from *Practise* question 2 to approximate the number of miles from the sun to each planet from the sun. Remember, Earth is approximately 150 million km from the sun.

Calendar and timetable problems

Learn

My brother's birthday is on 12th June. He was born in 2005.

How old was Nita's brother on 1st January 2012?

How old was he on 1st August 2012?

How precise can you be?

Practise

1 a Mateo starts to build a tree house on 26th March. He thinks it will take 17 days. When will he be finished?

   b It takes 35 days for a bean to grow into a beanstalk. If you planted a bean on 1st June, when will the beanstalk be fully grown?

   c Nita has six lessons, one a week, starting on 15th April. When is her last lesson?

   d Captain Samantha Cristoforetti, an Italian astronaut, went into space on 23rd November 2014 and returned on 11th June 2015. How long was she in space?

2 a Nita starts a journey at 18:00. It will take 2 hours and 45 minutes. When will she arrive at her destination?

   b Mateo spoke on the telephone to his friend for 40 minutes. If the call ended at 17:32, when did it start?

   c Nita arrives at a friend's house at 16:00 on Friday and stays until 9:30 on Sunday. How long has she stayed?

   d Mateo catches the 17:46 train for a journey of 30 minutes. Will he arrive before 6.30 pm?

3 Sir Isaac Newton was a physicist and mathematician.

   - He was born on 25th December 1642.
   - He died on 20th March 1727.

   How old was he when he died? Be as accurate as you can.

Solving puzzles and problems about time

Nita used sticks to show the time. How many sticks did she need?

Which other times could Nita make with the same digits?

1 Use sticks to make the digital digits 0–9.
Copy and complete this table:

Digital digit display	Sticks needed
0	
1	2
2	5
3	
4	
5	
6	
7	
8	
9	

2 How many different times can you make using:

a exactly 6 sticks   b fewer than 10 sticks.

3 Work out how many sticks you will need to write the time on each clock as a digital display.
Include two answers for a.m. and p.m. (using the 24-hour clock).

a    b

c    d

Which time in the 24-hour clock will require the most sticks?

What about in the 12-hour clock?

Self-check

A The metric system

1 Do these conversions.
   a 9.75 kg to grams
   b 0.57 m to centimetres
   c 0.75 l to millilitres

2 Convert these imperial measures to metric units.
   a 5 pounds
   b 10 pints
   c 22 lbs

B Length, area and perimeter

1 The perimeter of the blue square is 36 cm. Work out the area.

2 The area of the yellow rectangle is 36 cm². Work out the perimeter.

40 mm

C Time

1 A marathon runner starts the race at 11:00. It takes her three hours and 43 minutes to run the race. At what time did she finish?

2 How many weeks and days are there between 28th January and 2nd April?

3 Mateo's uncle is planning to visit Mateo. Use this bus timetable to answer the questions.

Stop 1, City Centre	17:08	17:18 *	17:28	17:38 *	17:48	18:08 *
Stop 2	17:33	17:43	17:53	18:03	18:13	18:33
Stop 3	17:43	17:53	18:03	18:13	18:23	18:43
Stop 4	17:58	--	18:18	--	18:38	--
* These services do not go beyond Stop 3						

a How long is the journey from City Centre (where Mateo's uncle works), to Stop 4, near Mateo's house?

b How long is the journey from City Centre to Stop 2?

c If Mateo's uncle can be at the City Centre bus stop at five past five, what time would he expect to arrive at Stop 4?

d If Mateo's uncle is at the City Centre bus stop at ten past five, when can he arrive at Stop 4?

e At what time can Mateo's uncle get to Stop 4 if he is at the City Centre bus stop at half past five?

Unit 13   Number and problem solving

13a Percentages

Explore

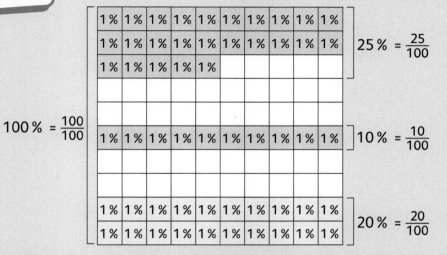

$$100\% = \frac{100}{100}$$

$$25\% = \frac{25}{100}$$

$$10\% = \frac{10}{100}$$

$$20\% = \frac{20}{100}$$

The word 'per cent' means per hundred. All percentages can be written with the denominator 100.

What other percentage and fraction equivalents can you find?

Can you simplify any of the fractions?

Key words

percentage

Finding percentages of amounts and shapes

Learn

You can use what you know about fraction and percentage equivalents to help find fractions of amounts or shapes.

50% is equivalent to $\frac{50}{100}$ or $\frac{1}{2}$, so you can find 50% by finding $\frac{1}{2}$.

10% is equivalent to $\frac{10}{100}$ or $\frac{1}{10}$, so you can find 10% by dividing by 10.

1% is equivalent to $\frac{1}{100}$, so you can find 1% by dividing by 100.

Look at this shape on the right. It has been divided into equal parts.

How many equal parts must be shaded each time so that 50% of the shape is blue, 10% of the shape is yellow, 5% is red and 20% is green?

Can you explain what percentage of the shape is left unshaded?

Practise

1 What fraction of each shape is shaded?

a

b

c

d

e Now write each fraction as a percentage.

2 Find the following percentages of these amounts:

a 10% of 150

b 20% of $300

c 25% of 240 g

d 5% of 40 litres

e 75% of $800

f Find the missing amounts.

10% of ☐ = 30

25% of ☐ = 100

1% of ☐ = 5

3 Nita's uncle is deciding which shop has the best deal on a new television.

	Shop A	Shop B	Shop C	Shop D
Usual price	$250	$200	$270	$280
Percentage discount	10% off	5% off	20% off	25% off
Discount in dollars	$25			
New price	$225			

a Complete the table for each shop to show the discount in dollars each time and the new price. Shop A has been done for you.

b Which shop has the best deal?

Try this

Nita and Mateo have been asking people to name their favourite sport.

a Nita asked ten people and three liked tennis best. What percentage is this?

b Mateo asked 20 people and also found three who liked tennis best. What percentage is this?

c When Nita and Mateo put all their results together, what percentage of people liked tennis best?

Think like a mathematician

Remember to use what you know about place value to help you divide by 10 or 100.

13b Ratio and proportion

Explore

I have less than $5 in my money box. I have three times as many 10c as 5c coins.

I have eight coins in my money box. One in every four coins is a 5c coin.

How much money could each child have in his or her money box?

What is the greatest and least amount that each child could have in his or her money box?

Ratio

Learn

Ratio is a way of comparing two quantities. You can use the language 'for every' to talk about ratio.

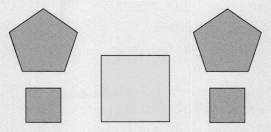

In this group of shapes, there are three squares for every two pentagons.
This ratio can be written as 3:2 (squares : pentagons) or as 2:3 (pentagons : squares)

Can you describe the ratio of green shapes to yellow shapes? And the ratio of large squares to small squares?

How many yellow shapes and green shapes will there be in two groups of these shapes?

Practise

1 Use the shape picture to complete this table about the ratio of pentagons to squares.

	1	2	4	40	80	800
Number of groups	1	2	4	40	80	800
Number of pentagons	2					
Number of squares	3					
Total number of shapes	5					

2 The ratio of boys to girls in a Maths class is 3 boys for every 2 girls (or 3:2)

a Are there more girls or boys in the class?

b If there are 30 children in the class, how many are boys and how many are girls?

c What would the ratio of boys to girls be if the number of boys and girls were equal?

Try this

a Write the recipe for a birthday party with 18 people.

b If the recipe uses 30 g of sugar, how many people will it serve?

Strawberry ice-cream

300g strawberries
90g sugar
250ml milk
250ml cream
1 vanilla pod
10 egg yolks
2 tablespoons lemon juice

Recipe for 6 people

Think like a mathematician

You can use your multiplication and division facts to help you work with ratio.

Proportion

Learn

Like fractions, we can use proportion to compare a part to the whole.

In this group of yellow and green shapes, two of the five shapes are pentagons.

Proportions are shown as fractions, so the proportion of pentagons in this group is $\frac{2}{5}$. What proportion of the group of shapes is yellow?

We can solve problems about direct proportion using multiplication and division to keep two or more quantities in the same ratio.

The total area of two small squares is 40cm². What is the total area of six of these squares?

Think like a mathematician

Remember that like fractions, proportions can also be shown in their simplest form or as equivalents e.g. $\frac{1}{2} = \frac{2}{4}$ and the fraction $\frac{5}{10}$ can be simplified to $\frac{1}{2}$.

Practise

1 Look at the picture.

What proportion of the whole group of flowers:

a is pink?

b has only one leaf on the stem?

c has more than four petals?

d has a blue centre ?

e has more than four petals, and two leaves on the stem?

2 A bunch of six flowers costs $1.50. How much will a bunch with eight of these flowers cost?

3 Sketch groups of circles and crosses to match these proportions. The first one has been done for you.

a $\frac{3}{5}$ of the group are circles. OOO✕✕

b $\frac{5}{8}$ of the group are crosses.

c $\frac{3}{4}$ of a group of 20 are crosses.

d $\frac{2}{3}$ of a group of 15 are circles.

e $\frac{3}{10}$ of a group of 20 are crosses.

⏻ 13c Multiplication and division

Explore

Nita and her dad are making a model sailing boat.

They are working on a scale of $\frac{1}{12}$, which means that every measurement will be $\frac{1}{12}$ of the size of the real boat.

The picture shows some measurements of the real boat.

How big will the model be?

6.72 m

1.8 m (width)

4.8 m

What if Nita and her dad work on a scale of $\frac{1}{6}$? Do you need to recalculate?

Try measuring some items in the classroom and then making a scaled drawing for each one that is $\frac{1}{6}$ of the size.

Using mental strategies to multiply and divide

> ## Learn
>
> What is the same and what is different about these arrays?
> What multiplications do they represent?
>
>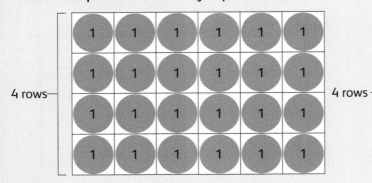
>
> The arrays show four rows of 6 and four rows of 0.6.
> These arrays can be written as 4 × 6 = 24 (24 lots of 1) and 4 × 0.6 = 2.4 (24 lots of 0.1).
>
> You can use your multiplication facts and place value to help you.
> For example: 0.6 is ten times smaller than 6, so the product of 4 × 0.6 is ten times smaller than the product of 4 × 6.
>
> You can check this using the inverse: 24 ÷ 4 = 6, so 2.4 ÷ 4 is ten times smaller, namely 0.6.

Practise

1 Use multiplication facts and place value to solve these calculations.

a	b	c
7 × 5 =	9 × 8 =	76 × 2 =
7 × 0.5 =	0.9 × 8 =	7.6 × 2 =
3.5 ÷ 7 =	7.2 ÷ 8 =	76 ÷ 2 =
3.5 ÷ 0.7 =	7.2 ÷ 0.8 =	7.6 ÷ 2 =

2 Find the missing numbers. Write the multiplication fact you used to help you each time.

a 8 × ☐ = 6.4   b ☐ × 0.7 = 4.2   c 1.2 × ☐ = 4.8   d 9.6 × ☐ = 19.2

e ☐ ÷ 8 = 0.8   f 4.2 ÷ ☐ = 0.6   g 4.8 ÷ 12 = ☐   h 1.92 ÷ 2 = ☐

3 Mateo builds a tower with small bricks. Each brick has a height of 1.1 cm.
What is the height of a tower made with:

a 2 of these bricks?   b 5 of these bricks?   c 12 of these bricks?

d The height of Mateo's tower is 9.9 cm. How many bricks did he use?

Learn

15 × 0.9

15 × 1.1

I want to use a multiplication fact and place value to help me but I don't know the answer to 15 × 9 and 15 × 11.

You could use a rounding and adjusting strategy to help you because 9 and 11 are very close to 10.

Can you remember how to use the rounding and adjusting strategy?

Practise

1 Use the rounding and adjusting strategy to help you complete these multiplications.

a	b	c	d
13 × 9	13 × 11	15 × 8	15 x 12
13 × 0.9	13 × 1.1	15 × 0.8	15 x 1.2

2 × 19   × 21   × 29   × 31

Choose a number from the box and a number to multiply it by to find a product that rounds to:

23	35	26	32
45	28	37	18

a 800 to the nearest 100.

b 400 to the nearest 100.

c 1100 to the nearest 100.

Think like a mathematician

When answering the questions in the *Practise* panel, remember to make an estimate first. This will save you from carrying out more calculations than you need.

Try this

Can you use what you know to help work out the answers to these calculations?

a 0.7 × 0.5 = ☐   b 0.42 ÷ 0.6 = ☐

c 0.8 × 0.6 = ☐   d 0.49 ÷ 0.7 = ☐

The relationship between fractions and division

The two arrays show the relationship between finding $\frac{1}{4}$ and dividing by four.
The same array can be used to find $\frac{3}{4}$ of 12. This is the same as finding $\frac{1}{4}$ of 12 and then multiplying this amount by three:

$\frac{1}{4}$ of 12 = 3

$\frac{3}{4}$ is the same as $\frac{1}{4} \times 3$, which is $3 \times 3 = 9$.

Can you explain how to find $\frac{2}{4}$ of 12?

What other fraction of 12 will give the same result? Why?

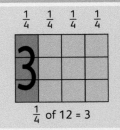

$\frac{1}{4}$ of 12 = 3

12 ÷ 4 = 3

Practise

1 a What does each array represent?
      Think about fractions for the first array
      and division for the second.

   b What is $\frac{2}{5}$ of 20? What is $\frac{3}{5}$ of 20?

2 Complete these calculations. The first one
   has been done for you.

   a $\frac{1}{10}$ of 120 = 120 ÷ 10   b ☐ of 500 = 500 ÷ 100

   c $\frac{1}{8}$ of 160 = ☐ ÷ 8   d ☐ of 240 = 240 ÷ 10

   e ☐ of 240 = 240 ÷ 6   f $\frac{1}{6}$ of 60 = 60 ÷ ☐

3 Find the fraction of each amount.

   a $\frac{3}{5}$ = of $300   b $\frac{3}{10}$ of $300   c $\frac{7}{100}$ of 1 000 g   d $\frac{7}{10}$ of 20 ℓ

   e $\frac{5}{8}$ of 320 m   f $\frac{9}{10}$ of 72 km   g $\frac{25}{100}$ of $20   h $\frac{5}{6}$ of 360 g

Try this

Nita measures the depth of a pool using
a stick. One quarter of the stick, a section
36 cm long, is above the water when the
end touches the bottom. How long is the
stick and how deep is the water?

Think like a mathematician

Remember to use what you know about
place value to help divide by 10 and 100.

Division and remainders

Learn

Look at the number **326** .

You know that $326 \div 4$ will leave a remainder because each of the three hundreds is divisible by four ($4 \times 25 = 100$), while 26 is not.

What other numbers can 326 be divided by that will definitely leave a remainder?
What divisibility tests can you use to help you?

$326 \div 4 = 81 \text{ r } 2$

You can use short division to show this.

$$\frac{8 \ 1 \ \text{r} \ 2}{4 \overline{)3 \, {}^3 2 \, 6}}$$

You can write the answer to this division as a mixed number by converting the remainder 2 to the fraction $\frac{2}{4}$ because $2 \div 4 = \frac{2}{4}$ (or two out of a group of four is $\frac{2}{4}$).

This can be simplified to $\frac{1}{2}$.

$326 \div 4 = 81\frac{1}{2}$

How can you write the mixed number $81\frac{1}{2}$ as a decimal?
What decimal equivalent can you use?

So $326 \div 4 = 81 \text{ r } 2$ or $81\frac{1}{2}$ or 81.5.

Dividing $326 \div 4$ will leave a remainder. Can you explain why?

Practise

1 Divide 326 by each of these numbers.
   Write your answers as a mixed number and as a decimal.
   a 10   b 100   c 5

2 Complete these divisions with money. How will you show any remainders? Why?

   a $ 325 \div 4$ b $ 770 \div 7$

   c $ 356 \div 8$ d $ 447 \div 5$

   e $ 667 \div 4$ d $ 447 \div 10$

3 Are these statements true or false?
Correct any statements that are false.

   a 725 ÷ 5 will divide exactly with no remainder.

   b 725 ÷ 25 will have a remainder.

   c 725 ÷ 4 will have a remainder that can be turned into the fraction $\frac{1}{4}$.

   d 723 ÷ 10 will have a remainder that can be turned into the decimal 0.03.

   e 723 ÷ 5 will have a remainder that can be turned into the fraction $\frac{2}{5}$.

4 Nita divides the number 565 by one of the numbers in the box.

   | 4 | 5 | 100 | 2 | 10 |

She writes her answer as a mixed
number and as a decimal.

□ $\frac{1}{2}$ and □.5

   a Which number(s) could Nita have
      used to divide 565 by? Show her actual
      calculation using short division.

   b Mateo divides 435 by a different
      number in the box. His answer is a
      number with two decimal places.
      What division did he carry out?

   c Write the answer to Mateo's calculation
      as a mixed number.

Try this

Nita is thinking of a number between 10
and 50.

This number is divisible by 5 but not by 10.

When this number is divided by 4, it leaves a
remainder that can be turned into the fraction $\frac{3}{4}$.

What could this number be? Is there more than
one possibility?

Think like a mathematician

Remember that all divisions can be written
as a fraction, so 1 ÷ 2 = $\frac{1}{2}$ and 3 ÷ 4 = $\frac{3}{4}$,
and so on.

Dividing numbers and sums of money by a two-digit number

Look at these two problems.
What is the same and what is different about them?

885 pencils are packed into boxes of 15.	$885 is split equally between 15 charities.
How many boxes of 15 pencils are there?	How much does each charity receive?

You can use the same methods to calculate the answer.
A long division method and a short division method are shown below.

How do these two methods work?

```
          5  9                      5  9
   15 | 8  8  5            15 | 8  ⁸8 ¹³5
15 × 5 → ( 7  5 )↓
          1  3  5
15 × 9 → ( 1  3  5 )
                0
```

What does the answer 59 represent for each of the original problems?

Try this

Find the missing digits to make this division correct.

```
       6 □
12 | 8 □ 6
    □ 2 ↓
      9 6
      9 6
        0
```

1 Complete these division calculations. Remember to make an estimate first.

   a 696 ÷ 12 =
      $696 ÷ 12 =
      696 cents ÷ 12 =

   b 407 ÷ 11 =
      $407 ÷ 11 =
      $4.07 ÷ 11 =

   c 555 ÷ 15
      $555 ÷ 15
      $5.55 ÷ 15

2 Solve each of these division problems.

   a How many games costing $12 can I buy for $552?

   b How many 15 cent lollipops did I buy for $3.90?

   c 264 people arrange themselves into groups of 11. How many groups did they form?

3 What is the value of one circle ⬤ each time?

   a

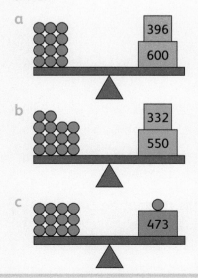

   b

   c

Using multiplication laws

Learn

Nita and Mateo are exploring different ways to calculate 45×32.
They record the three different methods they use.

What do you think they are doing each time? Why did they make these choices?

$$
\begin{aligned}
45 \times 32 &= 9 \times 5 \times 8 \times 4 \\
&= 9 \times 8 \times 5 \times 4 \\
&= 72 \times 20 \\
&= 72 \times 2 \times 10 \\
&= 144 \times 10 \\
&= ?
\end{aligned}
$$

$$
\begin{aligned}
45 \times 32 &= 90 \times 16 \\
&= 180 \times 8 \\
&= 360 \times 4 \\
&= 720 \times 2 \\
&= ?
\end{aligned}
$$

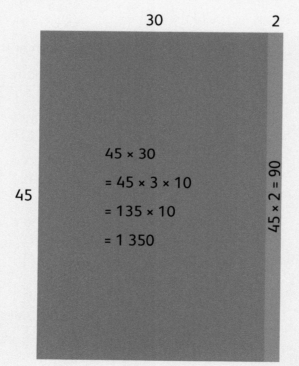

30   2

45

45×30

$= 45 \times 3 \times 10$

$= 135 \times 10$

$= 1\ 350$

$45 \times 2 = 90$

Can you use Nita and Mateo's recording to find the answer to 45×32?

Now look at this calculation: $45 \times 16 + 45 \times 16$

What do you notice?

Practise

1 Complete these calculations using some of the methods explored in the *Learn* section.
Be prepared to explain the choice you made.
Remember to make an estimate first.

a 8×76 b 25×17 c $15 \times 6 + 15 \times 4$

d 52×23 e $18 \times 15 + 5 \times 18$

2 The arrays show the start of the multiplication table for 14.
Use the arrays to complete these multiplication facts.
The first one has been done for you.

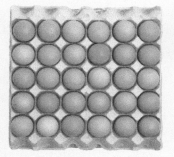

a $14 \times 1 = (10 \times 1) + (4 \times 1)$ b $14 \times 2 =$

c $14 \times 3 =$ d $14 \times 4 =$

e $14 \times 7 =$ f $14 \times 8 =$

g $14 \times 11 =$

3 Eggs are sold in large trays or in small boxes.

The cost of four large trays of eggs is the same as the cost of 19 small boxes of eggs.

Are these statements true or false? Correct any statements that are false.

a You get five more eggs for the same amount of money when you buy the four large trays.

b The number of eggs in eight large trays is equal to the number of eggs in 40 small boxes.

c Five large trays and five small boxes contain a total of 186 eggs.

d The number of eggs in 25 large trays is equal to the number of eggs in 125 small boxes.

e The cost of 24 large trays is the same as 115 small boxes.

Try this

Mateo and Nita's school organised a cross-country race for adults and children.
- The adults ran a 5-km course. 113 men and 137 women took part.
- The children ran a 1-km course. 57 boys and 43 girls took part.

How many kilometres, in total, were run that day?

Think like a mathematician

When deciding which method to use, look carefully at the numbers involved.

What do you notice about them? Can you reorder them or use factors to make the calculation easier? Don't forget that doubling and halving is a useful mental strategy.

Self-check

A Percentages

1 What percentage of this bar is shaded?

2 Answer these questions:
   a What is 10 % of 150?
   b What is $\frac{4}{25}$ as a percentage?
   c An electrical shop is offering a 20 % discount. If the cost of a computer was $280 before the sale, what does it cost now?

B Ratio and proportion

1 At a football game there are 100 spectators. Of those, 80 are fans of the home team and 20 are fans of the visiting team.
   a What is the ratio of home team fans to visiting team fans?
   b How many home team fans are there for every visiting team fan?
   c What proportion of the crowd is visiting team fans?
   d Four tickets to the game cost $120. How much do 10 tickets cost?

C Multiplication and division

1 Complete these calculations using your multiplication facts and place value.
   a 4.6 × 2   b 0.8 × 7
   c 5.6 ÷ 8   d 9.8 ÷ 4
   e 0.5 × 0.9

2 Which is larger: $\frac{3}{4}$ of 200 or $\frac{3}{4}$ of 180?

3 The local car wash makes $386 profit one Saturday.
   The team of four people shares the money equally between them.
   a Will they each receive a whole number of dollars?
      Use a test of divisibility to help you decide.
   b Calculate how much money each person receives.
   c The team used 252 litres of water during the 12 hours they cleaned cars that day.
      On average, how much water did they use each hour?

4 Which methods will you use to calculate these multiplications?
   Make an estimation and show the calculation you used each time.
   a 15 × 16
   b 138 × 3 + 138 × 2
   c 73 × 8
   d 63 × 24

14a   2-D shapes

Explore

In Morocco, walls are sometimes decorated with tiles in different patterns.

What kinds of polygons can you see in these tile examples below.

Key words

rhombus

Deducing properties of shapes

Learn

Here, four equilateral triangles have been combined to form two different shapes.

What properties do they share, and what properties are different?

I can calculate the interior angles of each shape without needing to measure. The second shape has two pairs of equal angles. Can you name it?

Practise

1 How many different shapes can you make by joining equilateral triangles?

   a Join 4 triangles.   b Join 5 triangles.   c Join 6 triangles.

   You can colour in on triangular paper, or cut out triangles using a template.

2 How many different shapes can you make where ...

   a all internal angles are equal?

   b two pairs of internal angles are equal?

   c one pair of internal angles is equal?

3 Copy this Venn diagram.

   Can you make a shape that would go in every section, just by joining equilateral triangles?

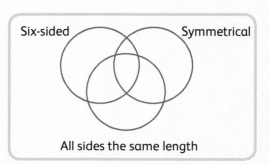

Six-sided   Symmetrical

All sides the same length

Try this

Make a template for a scalene triangle. Use this template to make new shapes by joining copies of the triangle. Can you make any new shapes with your scalene triangle that you could not make with the equilateral triangle?

Think like a mathematician

A kite has one pair of opposite equal angles, but a parallelogram has two pairs of opposite angles that are equal.

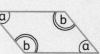

14b 3-D and 2-D shapes

Explore

What are the shapes that these crystals have formed?

Think like a mathematician

A 3-D shape that has only flat faces can be called a **polyhedron**. Each face of a polyhedron must be a **polygon**.

Key words

polyhedron

polygon

cross-section

Visualising and describing 3-D shapes

Learn

These are all nets of 3-D shapes.

a   b   c 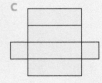 d 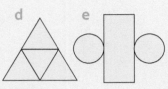 e f   g

 A cuboid has 3 pairs of parallel faces.

Would any of the faces be perpendicular?

Can you convince your partner that Nita's statement is correct and answer Mateo's question without making the actual shape?

Practise

1 Mateo makes a 3-D shape from each net. Which of the following statements is true about his new 3-D shape?

   a Shape (a) has many pairs of parallel faces.
   b Shape (f) has parallel edges.
   c Shape (f) has perpendicular edges.
   d Shape (b) has perpendicular edges.
   e Shape (g) and shape (c) have faces that are the same shape.
   f Shapes (a), (b) and (d) could all look like squares if you saw them from the right point of view.

2 Nita has made a shape by joining 4 cubes.

Mateo has made a different shape from 4 cubes.

Make these models from cubes and try to draw a net on squared paper that makes the same shape.

Try this

Mateo has made a shape. Design a net for this shape.

It might help to make the model then look at it from different angles.

Cross-sections and 3-D problems

Learn

A **cross-section** is the 2-D shape made by making a straight cut through a 3-D shape.

A prism can have the same cross-section cut from it again and again.

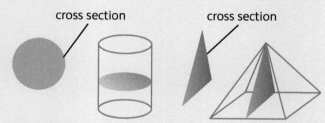

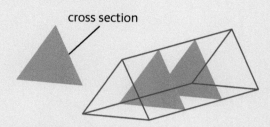

Practise

1   Which of these shapes have a triangular cross-section? Look at the diagrams in the *Learn* section to help you.)

   ● Cuboid

   ● Cone

   ● Tetrahedron

   ● Triangular prism.

2   Nita creates a prism. Its cross-section is a 2-D shape with exactly one pair of parallel sides. Sketch three different possible prisms that fit this description.

3   Nita places some solid shapes on paper and draws around their outlines. She turns each shape over onto each of its sides and draws those outlines too. Which shapes made these sets of outlines?

   a   Six squares

   b   A square and four triangles

   c   Two circles and a rectangle

   d   Four triangles

   e   Two triangles and three rectangles.

Try this

Mateo makes cubes from clay and slices through them to make different cross-sections.

Describe how he could make cross-sections that are:

a   square

b   rectangular (non-square)   c   triangular
d   pentagonal   e   hexagonal.

Is there more than one way to get each cross-section?

Think like a mathematician

Notice that, in some 3-D shapes, every face is the same polygon. These shapes look the same from any side. Some other shapes have more than one kind of face.

14c Angles in a triangle

Explore

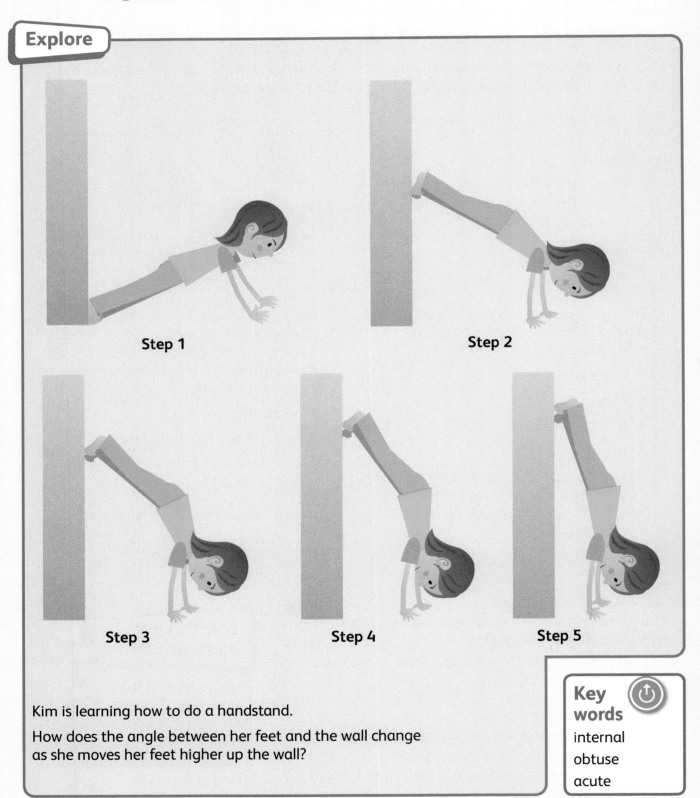

Step 1

Step 2

Step 3

Step 4

Step 5

Kim is learning how to do a handstand.

How does the angle between her feet and the wall change as she moves her feet higher up the wall?

Key words
internal
obtuse
acute

Acute and obtuse angles

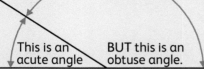

This is an acute angle

BUT this is an obtuse angle.

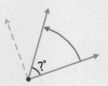

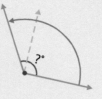

Estimate the number of degrees for each angle shown.

How many obtuse angles can any triangle have?

How many right angles or acute angles can any triangle have?

Practise

1 Sort these triangles into this Venn diagram.

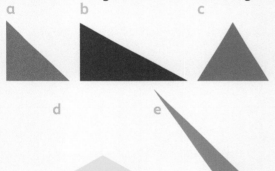

a   b   c

d   e

At least one obtuse angle

A   D   B   At least one acute angle

E   G   F

C   At least one right angle

2 Explain why no triangle can go in sections E or G.

3 Explain why section C cannot contain a triangle.

Think like a mathematician

It can help to turn the page when measuring angles in a triangle, so that the base of the protractor is easier to read.

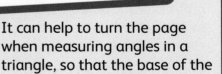

Try this

Draw two lines that are exactly 6 cm long and touch at one end.

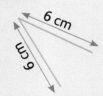

6 cm

6 cm

6 cm

6 cm

Then join up the two lines to form a triangle.

Measure all three internal angles. What do you notice?

Try this method to draw three different isosceles triangles.

14d Coordinates

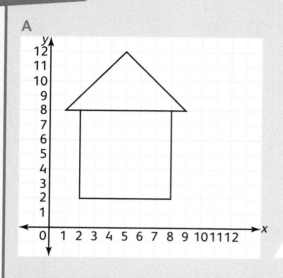

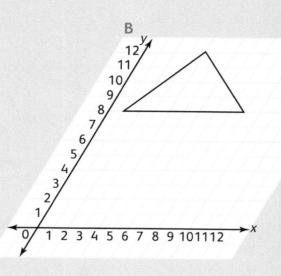

What would the square become on grid B?

Which coordinates would plot a square on grid B?

Reading and plotting coordinates

Learn

Although the grid lines are not shown on this coordinate grid, you can still work out the missing coordinates for the corners of the square.

Discuss two different ways of working out the missing coordinates of the bottom left-hand corner.

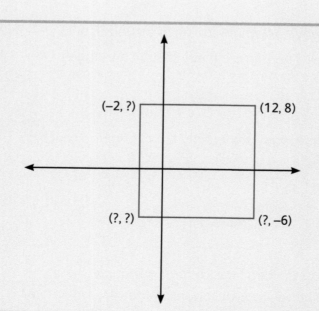

Practise

1 Mateo has labelled different points on this coordinate grid. One point has been labelled incorrectly.

a Can you see which point has the incorrect label?

b What mistake has been made?

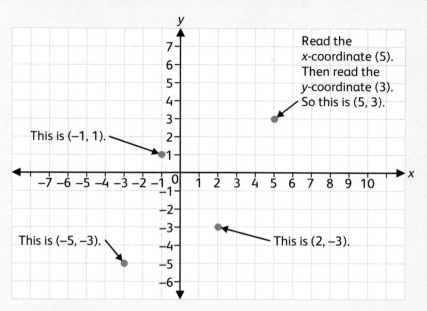

Read the x-coordinate (5). Then read the y-coordinate (3). So this is (5, 3).

This is (–1, 1).

This is (–5, –3).

This is (2, –3).

2 a Write the missing coordinates for the remaining corners of the square.

b Copy this table, and then sort these coordinates into the correct column.

(5, 15) (–15, 10) (0, 0) (25, –25) (–10, –5)
(25, –14) (–25, 15) (–30, –15)

The first one has been done for you.

Inside the square	Outside the square	On the perimeter of the square
(5, 15)		

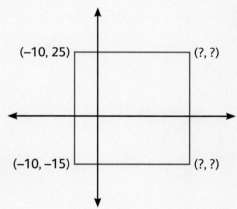

(–10, 25)   (?, ?)

(–10, –15)   (?, ?)

Try this

Use the information in this grid to find the coordinates for the corners A and B of this parallelogram.

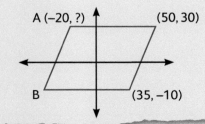

A (–20, ?)   (50, 30)

B   (35, –10)

177

14e Transformations

Explore

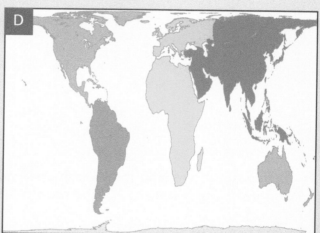

What is the same and what is different about each map?

Which map do you think is the most accurate? Why?

How might a scientist, a poet or a pilot respond to the different maps?

Transformations

Learn

Follow the steps to construct transformed shapes.

Measure where each corner will go, then join them up. Each corner moves in the same way.

Reflection

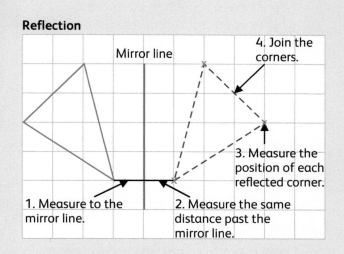

Mirror line

4. Join the corners.

3. Measure the position of each reflected corner.

1. Measure to the mirror line.

2. Measure the same distance past the mirror line.

Practise

Answer these questions about the rectangle ABCD.

1 What transformation could move point C to point one?

2 If ABCD is rotated 90° anticlockwise about A, where does point B go?

3 If ABCD is rotated 90° anticlockwise about B, where does point C go?

4 If ABCD is rotated 90° clockwise about B, which part of ABCD ends up at point 2?

5 If ABCD is reflected in the mirror line EF, where does point B go?

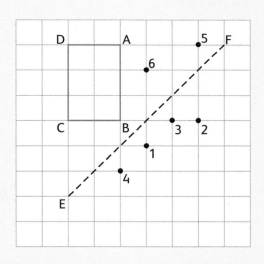

Try this

Can you reflect a P shape so that it looks like b, p, or q? Say where the mirror line would need to be.

Self-check

A 2-D shapes

1 Look at the shape and then read the statements below. Is each statement true or false? Give a reason in each case.

a It is not a quadrilateral.
b It has two equal sides.
c It has two equal angles.
d It has two parallel sides.
e It is a parallelogram.

B 3-D and 2-D shapes

1 A 3-D shape has all faces that are all the same shape. It has no parallel faces or perpendicular faces. It has a triangular cross-section.

a Write down at least one shape that this could be.
b Write down at least four shapes that it cannot be.

C Angles in a triangle

1 Draw a triangle that has an obtuse angle.

2 Draw a triangle that has a right angle.

3 Estimate the size of the other angles in each triangle, and then measure them with a protractor to check your estimates.

D Coordinates

1 Look at the map of Pirate Island and answer these questions:

a What is at (−3, 3)?
b Is the cave at (−7, 3)?
c What is at (8, −5)?
d Give the coordinates of the volcano.

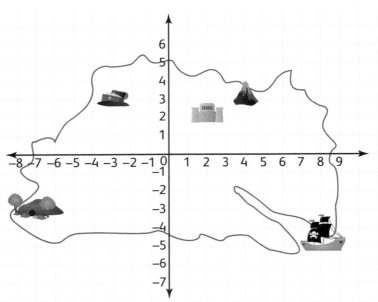

E Transformations

The triangle is reflected in the mirror line. What are the coordinates of the corners of the new shape?

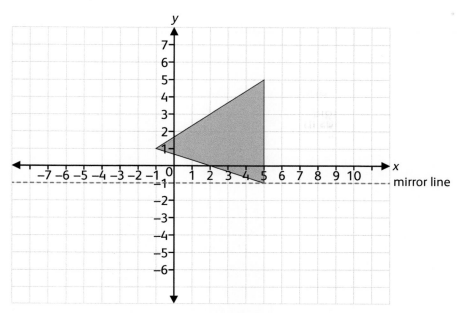

⏻ 15a Problem solving

Challenge 1

Caleb plans to build a tree fort.

Caleb is deciding which features his tree fort should have.

Flags?

A roof OR no roof?

Stairs or ladders?

Fun features?

Each tree fort has one feature from each category. So how many different tree forts can Caleb make? List all the possible combinations. Is there a faster way to work out all the different possibilities?

Challenge 2

1 Caleb has saved $25. His parents give him money in a ratio of 1:3 for every dollar he saves. How much money does he have in total?

2 Caleb wants the fort to have a roof, which is $40. The cost of the platform, wall and supports are already $32. He has also worked out the prices for the different features.

The climbing net price is half the cost of the slide minus $3.50.	A slide costs half the cost of the roof.	A fireperson's pole costs a fifth of the price of the slide.
A red and white flag costs three times the price of the white and black flag + 50 cents	A pirate flag is double the cost of the red and white flag.	The black and white flag costs $1.50.
A rope ladder costs a sixth of the price of the wooden stairs.	Wooden stairs cost $3.	Metal stairs cost triple the price of the rope ladder plus $1.

a Without working out the cost of each feature, which combination do you think will be the cheapest?

b Which features can Caleb afford on his budget? How many possible combinations are there now?

3 When Caleb and his mum arrive at the timber merchant, they see that the company is running a special offer, giving a 40% discount on wood.

a Which costs more now: the wooden or metal stairs?

b How does this change the budget for the wood for the tree fort? How much does he save?

c Which features can Caleb afford now with his savings?

d The ratio of rope to wood for the rope ladder is 3:2. The wood price has gone down by 40%, but the price of the rope has increased by 30%. Will the rope ladder now be cheaper or more expensive to make?

Challenge 3

Caleb and his mum are going to build this garden fort. Then, they are going to have a party to open it.

1 Caleb and his mum take some measurements and do calculations, to work out how much wood they need for the fort.

a The fort is 2.5 m long and 1.25 m wide. What is the area it covers?

b What is the perimeter of the floor?

2.5 m

1.25 m

c The walls will be made of upright planks that are 10.1 cm wide. How many planks are needed to make the walls?

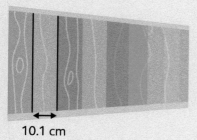

10.1 cm

d The floor of the fort will be 1 m above the ground and the walls will be 1 m high. The six corner posts are each 2.5 m long. How much of the posts will stick up above the walls?

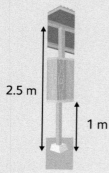

2.5 m

1 m

e A neighbour offers Caleb and his mum a board that measures 4 feet × 8 feet. Can this board be used to make the floor? Remember, 1 foot = 30.5 cm.

f Can Caleb and his mum use planks that are 4 inches wide to make the fort walls? Remember, 1 inch = 2.5 cm.

Challenge 4

1 The wood can be delivered on 30th May. After that, Caleb and his mum think they can do two hours of work on the fort every day until it is finished. Caleb's mum writes down how long they think each task will take. When will they be finished?

JUNE						
Sun	Mon	Tues	Wed	Thu	Fri	Sat
				1	2	3
4	5	6	7	8	9	10
11	12	13	14	15	16	17
18	19	20	21	22	23	24
25	26	27	28	29	30	

* Measuring out and putting in the posts – 2 hours

* Building the floor – 6 hours

* Building the walls – 6 hours

* Fitting on the roof – 1 hour

* Painting with 2 layers of paint – 2 x 2 hours with a five-hour gap between layers of paint

Challenge 5

1 When the fort is finished, Caleb has a sack relay race around the fort. In a sack relay race, you jump around one lap in the sack and then give the sack to the next person in line to jump. Here are the times that Caleb recorded on a stopwatch. The stopwatch measures seconds, tenths of seconds and hundredths of seconds. This means you can treat these numbers from the stopwatch like decimal numbers.

	Lion team	Tiger team
Lap 1	23.30	22.34
Lap 2	24.62	27.03
Lap 3	21.50	22.15
Lap 4	22.89	24.36

a Which team won?

b How many seconds did the winning team win by (to the nearest tenth of a second)?

c What was the total time for each team in minutes and seconds (to the nearest second)?

d Which team was ahead after Lap 1?

e Which team was ahead after Lap 2?

f For how many laps were Tigers ahead?

g One lap was 28 m. Each team raced four laps. How far did each team have to race?

h If the race carried on for 100 laps, approximately how long would it take? Give your time to the nearest minute.

i If the race was 100 laps, how many kilometres would each team have travelled?

j The lion and the tiger team ran a 5th lap. Now each team had the same mean time for a lap. Find 3 possible answers.

Challenge 6

1 After the race, the children use the sacks to make some letters. Work out the perimeter and area of these letters. Remember that they are made from sacks that are each 80 cm long and 50 cm wide.

a 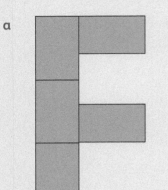   b 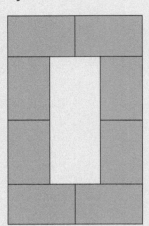   c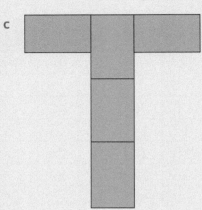

2 How could the children make the letter R to spell 'Fort?' (Think of how they could fold the sacks.)

3 Look at the letter O made from sacks (shown in question 1b).

   a What is the area of the 'hole' in the middle of the O?

   b Could this hole be filled with more sacks to make a solid rectangle, without any sacks being folded or overlapping? Explain your answer.

   c What is the smallest number of sacks that could be used to fill the hole completely?

Challenge 7

1 Caleb's uncle and aunt, who both live in other countries, want Caleb to show them the new fort. He will show them the fort by internet video call. His uncle is five time zones behind Caleb's time zone. His aunt is four time zones ahead.

   a When it is noon for Caleb, what time is it for his aunt? What time is it for his uncle?

   b Caleb's uncle suggests talking at noon his time. What time is that for Caleb? What time is that for Caleb's aunt?

   c When it is 1 p.m. for his aunt, what time is it for Caleb and his uncle?

   d They decide to do the video tour when it is 1 p.m. for Caleb. Caleb shows them around the new fort for 20 minutes. What time is it for his uncle and for his aunt when the tour is finished?

Mathematical dictionary

2-D A shape that has exacly **two** dimensions (such as width and height) and no thickness is 2-dimensional

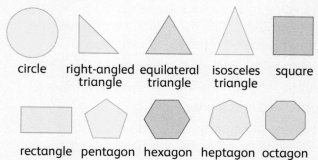

circle | right-angled triangle | equilateral triangle | isosceles triangle | square

rectangle | pentagon | hexagon | heptagon | octagon

some mathematical 2-D shapes

3-D Any object that has height, width and depth is 3-dimensional

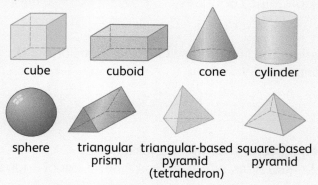

cube | cuboid | cone | cylinder

sphere | triangular prism | triangular-based pyramid (tetrahedron) | square-based pyramid

some mathematical 3-D shapes

A

acute angle an angle between 0° and 90°

adjust when you do calculations in your head, you often round off numbers to make the calculation easier and then you have to adjust the answer at the end

analogue clock a dial with hands used to show time; the dial shows 12 hours in a full circle; the minute hand moves 1 complete turn every circle

Analoaue clock

angle the amount of turn between 2 straight lines that meet at a point; usually measured in degrees; symbol: °

approximate, approximately almost; about; a number that is not exact, for example, 2 028 is approximately 2 000.

area the size of a surface; measured in 'square' units: mm², cm², m², km²

B

balance things are balanced when both sides have equal value, for example, 3 + 4 = 2 + 5 and 1 000 g = 1 kg

bar chart a chart that uses bars to show the relationship between groups of information

Cars in a car park

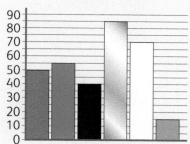

base the flat surface under a 3-D shape, for example, a square-based pyramid has 1 square base and 4 triangular faces

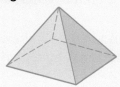

C

calendar a list of the days of the year, arranged by month, week and day

capacity the amount a container holds; it is measured in litres or millilitres, for example, the capacity of a 2 litre bottle is 2 litres

Celsius a scale used to measure temperature; sometimes called Centigrade; units are °C

centimetre a unit for measuring the length of something; 100 centimetre = 1 metre

century a period of 100 years

certain an event that has a very good chance of occurring

change the money left over when buying something with a note or coin bigger than the amount needed; the change is given back to the buyer

clockwise, anticlockwise clockwise: turning in the same direction as the hands on a clock; anticlockwise: turning in the opposite direction to the hands on a clock

clockwise   anticlockwise

common factor factors shared by two or more numbers

common multiple a multiple that is the multiple of more than one number

compound shape a shape made up by a number of other simple shapes

conversions changing one unit to another, for example, converting grams to kilograms

coordinates an ordered pair of (x, y) values that gives the position of a point on a graph

corner the point on a 2-D shape where two sides meet

cross-section shape that is shown when something is cut across by a plane

D

day a period of 24 hours

decade a period of ten years

decimal number a number less than 1; decimal numbers are shown by using a full stop, followed by tenths, hundredths, etc.; for example, 0.1 means one tenth

denominator a number below the line in a fraction, called the divisor, for example $\dfrac{2}{4}$

difference the answer you get when you subtract on number from another

digit the symbols 0, 1, 2, 3, 4, 5, 6, 7, 8 and 9; the value of each digit depends on its position, for example, in 16, the digit 1 represents one ten, while the 6 represents six ones

distance how far something is

divide to find how many times a number is contained in another number

divisible when a number can be divided without remainder; all even numbers are divisible by 2

double multiplying a number by 2

duration the length of time during which something continues

E

edge the line made where two faces of a 3-D shape meet

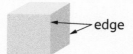

edge

equilateral triangle a triangle with 3 equal sides, which means it has 3 equal angles of 60°

equivalence another way of doing a calculation, but arriving at the same answer

equivalent the same value as

estimating to try to judge the value, size, amount, cost, speed, etc. of something without calculating it exactly

even number a number that is divisible by 2

event something that happens

exact the precise, accurate answer

F

face surface of a solid shape

factor a whole number that divides into another whole number exactly

factor pair two numbers that multiply to make a whole number; the two numbers are a factor pair

foot, feet an imperial unit of length, approximately 30 cm; 12 inches = 1 foot and 3 feet = 1 yard

fraction an equal part of something or a number, for example, $\frac{1}{2}$

1			
$\frac{1}{2}$		$\frac{1}{2}$	
$\frac{1}{4}$	$\frac{1}{4}$	$\frac{1}{4}$	$\frac{1}{4}$

G

gallon imperial unit for volume

generalisation a general statement that is true, based on facts

generated to produce or make

gram the basic unit for measuring weight in the metric system; 1 000 grams = 1 kilogram

greater than more than

H

hundredth one part of something that has been divided equally into a hundred parts or is shrunk to be 100 times smaller

I

imperial system of measurement used in the UK; still in use in some parts of the world

impossible cannot be done, cannot happen

improper fraction a fraction in which the numerator (the top number) is greater than or equal to the denominator (the bottom number), for example, $\frac{3}{2}$

infinitely without limit or end

inch, inches an imperial unit of length, approximately 2.5 cm; 12 inches = 1 foot

internal inside

isosceles triangle a triangle with 2 equal sides and so has 2 equal base angles. One of its angles can be a right angle (then it is called a right-angled isosceles triangle)

K

kilogram a measurement of weight; 1 000 grams

kilometre a measure of distance; 1 000 metres

L

less than smaller in size or number

likely probable; a good chance that something may happen

litre a measure or volume

M

mean a measure of average; mean = total of all data values ÷ number of data points

median the value that appears in the middle of a set of values when the values are arranged according to size or magnitude

metre a unit for measuring length or distance

metric unit any unit used to measure on a metric scale, for example, kilograms (kg), centimetres (cm), litres (l); all based on the decimal system

millilitre a unit for measuring volume; 1 000 millilitres = 1 litre

millimetre a unit for measuring length; 1 000 millimetres = 1 metre

million product of a thousand and a thousand; 1 000 000.

minute a unit for measuring time; 60 minutes = 1 hour

mirror line the central line over which you flip a shape when you create a mirror image

mixed number a number that consists of a whole number and a fraction or decimal, for example, $5\frac{3}{4}$ or 5.75

mode the value that appears most often in a set of data

multiple a multiple is the product of 2 numbers, for example, the multiples of 7 are 7, 14, 21, 28, and so on

multiply calculate the product of two numbers

N

near multiples a number that is almost the same as a multiple

negative numbers that are less than zero

net a two-dimensional pattern of flat shapes that can be folded to form a three-dimensional shape

A net

number bond an addition fact, for example, the number bonds for 10 are all pairs of whole numbers, like 2 and 8, which add up to 10

number facts see number bond

number line a line with points which represent numbers

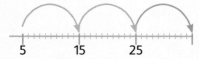

numerator the number above the line in a fraction that shows how many parts of the whole there are, for example $\frac{3}{4}$

O

obtuse an angle that is bigger than 90°.

odd number numbers that are not divisible by 2, for example, 1, 3, 5 and 7

opposite facing; for example, a side opposite another; the two sides are facing

ounce imperial measure of mass; symbol: oz; 1 ounce is approximately equal to 28 g; 16 oz = 1 pound

P

parallelogram a 2-D shape with four straight sides and two pairs of parallel lines

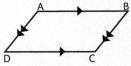

parallel lines two lines that are the same distance apart along their whole length

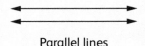

Parallel lines

part section

partition to break numbers up into different parts, for example, you could partition the number 43 512 into 40 000 + 3 000 + 500 + 10 + 2

percentage a number that is expressed as a fraction of 100, for example, if you score 70 % for a test, you score 70 out of 100

perimeter the distance around a two-dimensional shape

perpendicular lines lines that cut at 90°

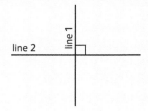

Perpendicular lines

pint imperial unit of volume

place value the value that every digit has in a number, for example, a one, a hundred or a thousand

polygon a 2-dimensional shape with three or more straight sides

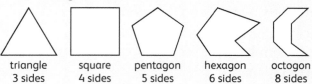

| triangle | square | pentagon | hexagon | octogon |
| 3 sides | 4 sides | 5 sides | 6 sides | 8 sides |

Examples of polygons

polyhedron a 3-dimensional shape whose faces are all polygons

pound imperial unit for weight

prime number a number with exactly two factors

probability how likely something is

proportion a comparison between two numbers showing their relationship in terms of size, amount, position, etc.; proportions are shown as fractions

protractor mathematical instrument used for measuring angles

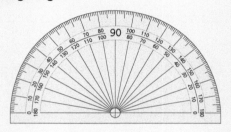

Q

quadrant one of the 4 quarters formed by the x-axis and y-axis on a graph

quadrilateral 2-D shape that has four straight sides

R

ratio a relationship between two amounts, for example, there are 12 boys for every 15 girls, the ratio is 12 to 15 or 12 : 15

recombine putting together again

rectangle a quadrilateral with four right angles

reflected when an object is flipped to create a mirror image; each point of that mirror image is exactly the same distance away from the central line, called the mirror line, as the original object, but it is on the opposite side of the line

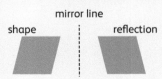

mirror line
shape   reflection

reliable can be trusted; always correct

remainder the amount left over after division

rhombus a quadrilateral with four sides of equal length

rotated turn on an axis

rounding to make a number simpler, but keep its value close to what it was

rule a set pattern or law that must be followed

S

scale the ratio between the real object and a drawing of the object

seconds unit of time; 60 seconds = 1 minute

sequence a list of numbers in which each number is obtained according to a specific rule

simplify to write something in its simplest form

square a rectangle with edges all the same length

symmetry a shape has symmetry if you can draw one or more lines of symmetry (mirror lines) through it; each half on either side of the line would look exactly the same if viewed in a mirror

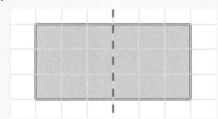

systematic done according to a fixed plan or system

T

tenth one part of something that has been divided equally into ten parts or ten times a hundred

term number sequences follow a rule that connects each value within them. These values are called terms. Example, when you count 0, 1, 2, 3, 4 … the sequence of numbers follows the rule that the next term is always one more than the previous term

time zone a part of the world that observes a standard time; there are nine time zones in the world

timetable any plan or schedule showing the times at which certain things will happen

Bus station	08:56	12:11	15:26	18:41
City centre	09:10	12:25	15:40	18:55
Railway station	09:22	12:37	15:52	19:07
Airport	09:37	12:52	16:07	19:22
Airport	09:43	12:58	16:13	19:28
Railway station	09:53	13:08	16:23	19:38
City centre	10:03	13:18	16:33	19:48
Bus station	10:20	13:35	16:50	20:05

total sum

trapezium a quadrilateral with one pair of parallel lines

transformation when you move a shape so that it is in a different position

translation when you move a shape along a straight line without changing the way it looks, for example, you can move it up and down, left or right

triangle a 2-D shape with 3 sides

U

unlikely not a very good chance of happening

V

vertex (plural: vertices) the point at which two or more flat lines meet to form an angle, corner

volume the amount of liquid in a container, for example, 1 litre of water in a 2 l bottle; measured in millilitres and litres; see capacity

W

week time period; 7 days

whole number a number that does not have fractions or decimals

X

x-axis the horizontal axis of a coordinate grid

Y

y-axis the vertical axis of a coordinate grid

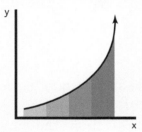

yard an imperial unit of length; 1 yard is approximately equal to 90 cm; symbol: yd; 36 inches = 3 feet = 1 yard

year time period; 52 weeks